THE GIFT OF LIFE

A theological commentary on the "Instruction on Respect for Human Life in its Origin And on the Dignity of Procreation: Replies to Certain Questions of the Day." (Congregation for the Doctrine of the Faith, 22 February 1987)

by
Rev. David Q. Liptak
with
Medical Notes and Glossary
by
Leo T. Duffy, M.D.

Foreword
by
Most Rev. Daniel P. Reilly, D.D.
Bishop of Norwich

Introduction
by
Rev. Ronald Lawler, O.F.M., Cap., Ph.D.

To Mary, Mother of God, and
Sedes Sapientiae.
With Heartfelt Thanks for
Pope John Paul II,
This Marian Year, 1987-88

IMPRIMATUR
+ Most Rev. John F. Whealon, D.D.
Archbishop of Hartford

The Nihil Obstat and Imprimatur are official declarations that a book or pamphlet is free from doctrinal or moral error. No implications contained therein that those who have granted the Nihil Obstat and Imprimatur agree with the contents, opinions or statements expressed.

27 July 1987

Copyright © 1988 by Liturgical Publications, Inc., 1937 10th Avenue North, Lake Worth, Florida 33461. All rights reserved. No part of this book may be reproduced or transmitted in any form or by any means, electronic or mechanical, including photocopying, recording or by any information storage and retrieval without permission in writing from the Publisher.

ISBN: 0-940169-06-1

Table of Contents

Foreword by Most Rev. Daniel P. Reilly, D.D.,
   Bishop of Norwich ix
Introduction by
   Rev. Ronald Lawler, O.F.M., Cap., Ph.D. xi
Author's Preface xiii
Part One, The Theological Commentary
   A Vision of Man 1
   The Body-Soul Union 5
   Some*one*, Not Some*thing* 9
   On Conjugal Union 13
   Creatures Are Not Gods 17
   Procreation, Not Reproduction 21
   Experimenting In General 25
   Therapeutic Experimentation
     (Prenatal Testing) 29
   Nontherapeutic Experimentation 33
   'Freezing' and Manipulating Embryos 37
   Artificial Forms 41
   Heterologous Conception 45
   "Surrogate" Motherhood 49
   Homologous Conception 53
   Treating Sterility 57
   A New Procedure "LTOT" 61
   Needed Legislation 63
   Extracorporeal Embryos and Laws 67
Part Two, The Medical Commentary
   Foreword by Leo T. Duffy, M.D. 73
   Chapter I: Procreation 75
   Chapter II: Abortion 97
   Chapter III: Genetics 105
   Chapter IV: Experimentation 117
   Glossary of Terms Used 127
   Syndromes 147
Bibliography 149

Foreword

Almost as soon as it was issued, the Holy See's *Instruction on Respect for Human Life in its Origin and on the Dignity of Procreation* was met with much questioning and sometimes disdain in the media. An article in *Newsweek* (March 23, 1987, pp. 42-43) entitled "Rules for Making Love and Babies" did not hesitate to conclude that "the Vatican appears to be more intent on repeating past papal dicta than rethinking its moral principles." Yet, this same article did give a cautious nod to the ever growing danger of "scientific indifference to human life at its origin."

In view of this confusion, Father David Liptak and Dr. Leo T. Duffy do us an immense service by reviewing the background to this most important *Instruction*. Rooted in the teachings of Vatican II, and presenting what might be called a "personalist" philosophy of humanity as well as insisting upon the essential unity of body and spirit by way of St. Thomas Aquinas, our authors remind us of the fundamental truths expressed in the *Instruction*, namely, that human life is sacred and indeed that the body must be viewed with reverence. By examining these truths, our authors clearly demonstrate that this *Instruction*, far from being a throw-back, is instead a beautiful affirmation of both the dignity of humanity and of the God-given gift of the conjugal union. Once again we see that Christ's wisdom, tested by the centuries, has much to say to the human family as it faces the moral challenges of modern technology. It is my hope that this book will be widely read and will further the "Good News" of Our Lord Jesus Christ, who by His Redemptive Act has given to each and every human being an infinite worth.

The Most Reverend Daniel P. Reilly
Bishop of Norwich
11 September 1987

Introduction

Today we hear much of artificial ways of producing children. First there was artificial insemination. Later we heard of *in vitro* ("in glass") fertilization. Then we learned of the freezing and transplanting of human fetuses. Surrogate motherhood became an object of media concern.

More startling things were spoken of. If we are to produce rather than beget children, perhaps we can exercise "quality control," and by genetic manipulation shape "better" kinds of babies.

On February 22, 1987, the Holy See published an important *Instruction* ("The Gift of Life") to cast the light of faith on the questions that arise out of the new technologies of conception.

Christian faith sees great wisdom and beauty in the original divine plan for calling new human beings into existence. Faith believes that each new person should be "begotten, not made." Each one of us should be able to rejoice that we were summoned into existence both by an act of God's love and by an act of interpersonal love of a father and a mother.

Certainly it is easy to understand why technological forms of generation seem attractive to many. Yet adoption of them is a radical change in basic approaches to human life. To adopt them is to adopt a moral stance that cannot easily be reconciled with all that human dignity requires, or Judaeo-Christian morality proclaims.

Father David Liptak is a splendid theologian, and a gifted writer. Doctor Leo T. Duffy is a physician able to explain clearly the medical and scientific aspects of the questions involved. Together they have written a book well worth the attention of those concerned with one of today's most pressing questions.

> Rev. Ronald Lawler, O.F.M., Cap., Ph.D.
> Director, Institute for Advanced Studies
>   in Catholic Doctrine
> St. John's University, Jamaica, New York
> Solemnity of the Assumption of Mary, 1987

Author's Preface

The magnificent heritage of our Catholic Moral Tradition shines forth with extraordinary brilliance in the "Instruction on Respect for Human Life in Its Origin and on the Dignity of Procreation: Replies to Certain Questions of the Day" issued by the Congregation for the Doctrine of the Faith on 22 Feb., 1987.

IT IS a source of pride to know that we live within a Church that can speak for Christ authoritatively on complicated, profound, ethical questions; within a Church that in fact does speak for Christ firmly, unequivocally, enlightenedly and courageously, despite the errors and confusions in which so many academics, journalists, and unfortunately, some theologians and clerics are immersed, almost as in a labyrinth.

THIS our historic Roman Church is not intimidated by surveys which presume to determine ethics, or so-called "expert" opinions, ambiguities or rejections. It speaks rather from a font of wisdom drawn from the Sacred Scriptures and Tradition, and with a consistency that can be traced back to the very beginning, when Christ our Lord brought the moral law to perfection with his law of love. This wisdom can withstand any assault leveled against it, any attempt to undermine it, any effort to ridicule it.

JUST A QUICK reading of the new "Instruction," prepared by the Congregation for the Doctrine of the Faith (whose prefect is one of the world's towering theologians) and approved by Pope John Paul II (himself "the greatest moral leader of our century," as Billy Graham has said), rekindles our appreciation of the rich ethical treasures we possess: the dignity of the human person, unique, precious and unrepeatable; the holiness of human life from the moment of conception, the sanctity of *procreation* (not simply "reproduction"), of human sexuality, of marriage.

THESE PERENNIAL biblical values help us solve existential bioethical questions. What the Church has just reaffirmed reflects eternal values that have already been related to new bioethical problems by our finest Catholic moral theologians; in this country, Father Ronald Lawler, for example, and Dr. William E. May, and Father Edward Bayer, to name just a few.

In some quarters intense opposition to the Vatican Instruction has been expressed. But even this should be the occasion for appreciation on our part. It means that the Church's position is perceived as clear and firm. If some are challenging it, this means that after all else is said, they are in quest, at least interested enough in a moral position to speak or write about it. What other Church or religious body today generates so much interest in its moral teaching? Whatever else, the Church is perceived at least as not fearful of taking a moral position: that, moreover, its moral position cannot change. That, too, its moral position serves the *person*.

We are reminded of G.K. Chesterton's remark that what the world needs most today is not a Church that is right when the world is right, but a Church that is right —*and certain that it is right* — when the world is wrong.

The first portion of this manual, from my pen, constitutes a theological survey of the Vatican's Instruction and a brief analysis and application of its principles.

It largely reflects a series of columns I wrote for The Catholic Transcript (Hartford) in 1987. The second half contains the medical aspects and includes a glossary of terms, the work of Dr. Leo T. Duffy, Medical Consultant to the Pope John Paul II Bioethics Center, located at Holy Apostles Seminary in Cromwell, CT.

We are indebted to many persons for helping us put together this manuscript. Special thanks are due to the Most Rev. John F. Whealon, D.D., Archbishop of Hartford; the Most Rev. Daniel P. Reilly, D.D., Bishop of Norwich and Chancellor of Holy Apostles Seminary; the Very Rev. Francis J. Lescoe, Ph.D., President and Rector of Holy Apostles and Co-Director of the Pope John Paul II Bioethics Center there; the Rev. Ronald Lawler, O.F.M., Cap., Ph.D., Director of the Institute for Advanced Studies in Catholic Doctrine at St. John's University, Jamaica, New York, and one of America's leading moral theologians; the Rev. Joseph P. LoCigno, Ph.D., S.T.D., Senior Editor of Liturgical Publications; and Attorney Joseph Nucera, J.D., Legal Consultant to the Pope John Paul II Bioethics Center.

The text of the Vatican Instruction used for this Commentary is that published in the English version of *L'Osservatore Romano*, issue of 16 March 1987 (N.11:979).

> Rev. D.Q. Liptak
> 25 July 1987
> Feast of St. James, Apostle

A Vision of Man

The "Instruction on Respect for Human Life in its Origin and on the Dignity of Procreation," issued by the Congregation for the Doctrine of the Faith with the approval of Pope John Paul II on 22 February 1987, the Feast of the Chair of St. Peter the Apostle, and presented in the Press Office of the Holy See on 10 March, opens with the words (in English) "The gift of life . . ." These words set the theme for the entire document, a compellingly beautiful and relevant witness to the Church's perennial defense of human life at its beginnings, and of the mystery of human procreation.

Not meant to be a thorough and systematic doctrinal and theological survey regarding incipient human life and procreation, it is rather a Catholic response to some inquiries pertaining to new bioethical processes generally categorized under such headings as technological reproduction, genetic engineering, and fetal experimentation.

SUCH QUESTIONS, theologian Cardinal Joseph Ratzinger, Prefect of the Congregation for the Doctrine of the Faith, explained in an intervention during the Vatican press conference of 10 March, had been put to the Holy See not only by various episcopal conferences, individual bishops and theologians, but also by physicians, scientists and marrieds. The answers provided in the Instruction, he explained, represent the fruit of widespread consultation and of long and profound study within the context of the Church's anthropology; namely, "a vision of man, of his nature and dignity, of his origin and destiny" that reflects the Bible and Sacred Tradition as conveyed by the Church's teaching authority known as the Magisterium (See *L'Osservatore Romano*, English edition, 16 March 1987, p. 8)

SPECIFICALLY, what is this vision of man? Cardinal Ratzinger reaffirmed that it entails three theses: 1) the human body is a constitutive part of the human person and expresses itself through it; 2) the human person is endowed with such a dignity that he or she can never be dismissed merely as a "thing," an "object"; on the contrary, the human person must always be acknowledged as a "subject" — "some*one*" and not "some*thing*"; 3) the only act which, of its very nature, is ethically worthy to place the conditions for the conception of a new human life, is the conjugal act. (Ibid.)

SINCE human beings are *subjects* and not objects, they are meant to be *begotten*, not made. They are not products, but *persons*.

THESE THREE theses ground "The Gift of Life" and permeate it. "In an easily pragmatic and utilitarian cultural context which values the morality of human actions solely on the basis of their results," Cardinal Ratzinger added, "it is essential to have ethical reflection capable of showing the reducible originality of moral good and that it is rooted in the entire truth about the human person which reason, enlightened by faith, discovers. It is the task of moral theology to show that the existence of moral norms, having a precise unchangeable and unconditional content, is the sole guarantee for the respect and full realization of man in his truth." (Ibid.)

WHEN ANTHROPOLOGY is faithful to the Christian fonts of morality, the Cardinal concluded his intervention, mankind is ensured of the possibility of living and loving in that dignity and freedom which derive from reverence for the truth. Moreover, in this process moral theology itself refines its identity and its value, since working for man's defense and progress, for his eternal salvation, and, ultimately, for the glory of God, is the meaning and goal of all moral endeavor — of all human endeavor.

The Body-Soul Union

The first of three theses pertaining to the vision of man reflected in the Instruction on the gift of life and the sanctity of procreation, is an affirmation of the substantial unity of the human person.

THIS IS a thesis not sufficiently considered, much less appreciated, in the contemporary world, so that it must be restated time and time again. As Cardinal Joseph Ratzinger explained in his intervention during the 10 March press conference in Rome announcing the new document, the human body "is a constitutive part of the human person which manifests and expresses itself through it. Thanks to the union with the spirit, the body is the manifestation of the person itself. It can also be said that the body is the person itself in its visibility."

PLATONIC dualism — the theory that soul and body are clearly separable entities — is at issue here. The Greek philosopher Plato (347 B.C.) taught that the soul was "in" the body in roughly the same manner that a pilot is in his ship. Plato's successor, Aristotle (d. 322 B.C.), moved to correct this concept by focusing on the essential unity of body and spirit. Centuries later, St. Thomas Aquinas, resting his argumentation largely on Aristotle, analyzed the body-spirit relationship in terms of the unity of both. (See his *Summa Contra Gentiles*, II. c. 68.) The Church utilized Aquinas' analysis when it defined the soul as the substantial form of the human body (Council of Vienne, 1312; DS 902)

TO EXPRESS this another way, the human soul is not just a spiritual substance making use of a body. To be a human being, theologian Romano Guardini once put it, "is to be spirit expressed and made active through the body." (in *The Last Things*, University of Notre Dame Press, 1965, p. 61)

TO RELATE all this to each person's origins, St. Thomas held that the soul shares its being with the body. One of Aquinas' finest interpreters in this century, Etienne Gilson, explained that the soul "receives the body in the communion of its own act of being . . . Were it not so, the whole being of man would not be one and the unity of man would not be a substantial unity . . ." (in *The Elements of Christian Philosophy*, Doubleday, 1960; pp. 228-229)

THE LUBLIN Personalists summarize this teaching thus: "The human soul, having an actual relation to matter, is expressed through the body organized for the soul." (in *I-Man*, by M. Krapiec, English translation. Mariel Pub. 1983, p. 429)

ALL OF THE above means that one cannot realistically say, for example, "This is my body; I can do with *it* as I please." A similar protestation is made by some pro-abortion women's groups; "It's my body; consequently I can have an abortion if I so decide." (Here, of course, the situation is further complicated, since the protest alleges that the child in the womb is nondistinct from the mother's own body. In truth, another human being, body-soul composite, is involved.)

BECAUSE the human person is a unity of spirit and body, the body is viewed by the Church with reverence. Indeed, there is an ancient adage, attributed to the Latin lawyer-apologist Tertullian (d. 230) that the body is the doorway to salvation (*caro cardo salutis*). Whereas the human body can be studied merely scientifically as a complex of tissues, organs and functions, nonetheless, in Cardinal Ratzinger's words — "from the metaphysical and theological aspect it appears essentially different; it belongs to a level of being which is qualitatively superior." Hence "the respect due to the person should be expressed as well in respect for the human body by means of which the person expresses it." (in Press Conference, 10 March)

THE BOTTOM LINE is that the human body is not to be treated as an object, a thing that can be used or manipulated. Moreover, any inadequate view of the body inevitably leads to an inadequate view of the person.

Some*one*, Not Some*thing*

The second thesis pertinent to the Instruction on the gift of life and the sanctity of procreation, Cardinal Joseph Ratzinger pointed out during the press conference presenting the new document on 10 March, really grounds the first one (the unity of soul and body). It is one which the Church, he said, cannot restate too often; namely, that the human person can never be considered simply as an "object," but must always be viewed as "subject."

PUT SIMPLY, this is to say that the human being is always "some*one*, and never "some*thing*."

TO RELATE this immediately to technological reproduction: reproductive techniques constitute a "production of objects." This is apparent from the fact that the logic of many of these techniques *per se* institutes "a relationship of inequality between the technician (who produces) and that which is produced, and therefore it is also a relationship of dominion of the one over the other."

TO GRASP the unacceptability of this logic, the Cardinal continued, "we must free ourselves from one of the most sinister convictions which this very 'technology' has introduced into our consciences"; specifically, the idea that reality does not possess any truth of its own; on the contrary (this erroneous idea goes on), it is the human *intention*, and the human intention *alone* that gives ontological (real) significance to everything.

A DRAMATIC example as to how this conviction is evidenced in contemporary bioethics is seen in spouses whose *desire* to have a child, plus the intention of researchers to augment their knowledge (for prospective benefits), is translated into the norm that "whatever is technically possible is also morally permissible."

WHILE insisting upon an objective moral order in assessing the morality of human acts, the Church does have — in the Cardinal's words — "a deep understanding of the legitimate aspirations of spouses to see expressed in a child the sign of their conjugal love." Too, the Church does appreciate "the efforts of medical research" oriented toward cure of conjugal sterility. Such efforts are welcomed *if and when they fully safeguard the dignity of human procreation.*

AGAIN, HOWEVER, *the uprightness of the end and the goodness of the intentions on the part of those involved do not of themselves suffice to render as morally permissible* recourse to any or all means of technological reproduction available today.

FOR THIS REASON, the Cardinal argues, the Church's Magisterium "cannot make even the slightest compromise with a viewpoint in which subjective desire is the sole and sufficient criterion to legitimate any medical intervention whatsoever."

HERE the Cardinal adds that certain solid thinkers of the present day, although they proceed from different premises than those of the Church, have also voiced concern over "the essentially antihuman character of the productive-technological mentality."

IN THE last analysis, then, the key moral question reads like this: "What is the act that of its very nature is ethically worthy to place the conditions for the conception of a new human person?"

THE CHURCH'S considered response is encapsulated in the third and last thesis upon which the Vatican's Instruction rests.

INCIDENTALLY — but this seems almost unnecessary to point out — what we are dealing with in the Vatican Instruction on the gift of life and the sanctity of procreation is a profound, complex, tightly reasoned, and sensitively expressed theological masterpiece, one so characteristic of Pope John Paul II, *the* Ethician of Lublin, and Cardinal Ratzinger, also one of the world's most prestigious theologians. This kind of substantial theologizing (as contradistinguished from that being done by some academics or clerics for popular consumption in the media) requires an approach with a serious and genuinely searching mind, as well as a heart ready to set aside current popular prejudices and shallow arguments, and literally join in the arduous, often slow-going, frequently steep and agonizing ascent to truth, an ascent which involves falling upon our knees from time to time to remove obstacles and "turning over rocks," as it were, to make the passage safer; as well as trudging onward with determination.

On Conjugal Union

The final anthropological-ethical thesis integral to the argumentation of the Vatican's Instruction on the gift of life and the sanctity of procreation is, in Cardinal Joseph Ratzinger's words during his intervention at the press conference on 10 March, that "only the conjugal act is worthy to place the conditions for the conception of a new human person."

THIS THESIS follows from the overall Christian vision of human sexuality, a highly sophisticated, biblically based vision magnificently articulated by Vatican Council II in the Pastoral Constitution on the Church in the Modern World (*Gaudium et Spes*); by Pope Paul VI in his encyclical *Humanae Vitae*; and by John Paul II in his Apostolic Exhortation, *Familiaris Consortio*, as well as in his frequent Wednesday catecheses.

CONJUGAL SEXUALITY constitutes the expression of definitive spousal self-donation, and thereby sustains and strengthens a total and an indissoluble communion of love between the spouses. "It is through this, its intimate truth," Cardinal Ratzinger reaffirmed, "that conjugal sexuality is called, precisely in the specific conjugal act of the union of the spouses, to a 'certain participation in God's creative work.'" (*Gaudium et Spes*, n. 50)

"UNION OF the spouses" and a "certain participation in God's work": this means that these two fundamental elements are included in the conjugal act. In traditional Catholic doctrine we speak of the procreative (i.e., the life-giving) meaning of conjugal communion, and the unitive (i.e., love-giving) meaning of conjugal communion. In *Familiaris Consortio*, Pope John Paul II explains that these two *meanings* are placed by the Creator into the very *language* of the conjugal act; indeed, man cannot deliberately separate them without making conjugal union something it was never meant to be. Earlier this principle was enunciated in Section 12 of *Humanae Vitae* by Pope Paul VI.

WHENEVER sexual union is considered, therefore, the moral law requires that the procreative aspect be not separated from the unitive.

IN TECHNOLOGICAL reproduction, however, whether it be artificial insemination (AI) or *in vitro* fertilization (IVF) or surrogate parenting, or some future prospect of asexual reproduction (e.g., cloning), the procreative and the unitive aspects of sexual union are in fact sundered, as a result of which children are conceived in the context of *production* rather than *generation*. To put this positively, in Cardinal Ratzinger's words:

"THE CONJUGAL ACT, in which are placed the conditions for the beginning of new life, does not create any relationship of 'production' between parents and children; by it the child is *generated*, not produced. The spouses place an act of love in the reciprocal gift of themselves and the child that can arise from this act is the gift of God's creative love. He or she is entrusted to the parents to be received by them with gratitude and infinite respect."

EACH and every human being is a *person, not an object*. The only "cradle" worthy of the new human being is the conjugal act, by which spouses specifically express their communion of interpersonal love.

WHAT CARDINAL Ratzinger explained in this regard is at the heart of Pope John Paul II's often repeated doctrine to the effect that every single human being, from the moment of conception, is not a thing, *but a "Thou,"* who is unique, precious and unrepeatable. The theistic existential philosophers have also argued this strongly from the existential viewpoint; the Jewish thinker, Martin Buber, for example, in his epoch-making book *Ich-du* (1923), and the French Catholic philosopher, Gabriel Marcel, who actually pioneered the concept. (See *Existentialism With or Without God*, by Francis J. Lescoe, Alba House, 1974, pp. 156 sqq.). M. Buber magnificently demonstrated that the Divine "Thou" constitutes the basis of every "I-Thou" relation. (See *I-Man*, abridged version, by Francis J. Lescoe and Roger B. Duncan, Mariel Pub., 1985, p. 204.)

Creatures Are Not Gods

The Vatican's Instruction on the gift of life and the sanctity of human procreation appears in five sections: 1) a formal Introduction which rehearses fundamental moral principles relevant to bioethical aspects of the origin of life and procreation; 2) Part I, entitled, "Respect For human embryos"; 3) Part II, "Interventions upon human procreation"; 4) Part III, "The values and moral obligations that civil legislation must respect and sanction in this matter"; and 5) a brief "Conclusion."

THE INTRODUCTION opens with a memorable sentence: "The *gift* of life which *God the Creator* and Father has *entrusted* to man *calls* him to *appreciate* the *inestimable value* of what he has been given and to take *responsibility* for it: this fundamental principle must be placed at the center of one's reflection in order to clarify and solve the moral problems raised by artificial interventions on life as it originates and on the processes of procreation." (*L'Osservatore Romano*, English edition, 16 March 1987, p. 1; italics added)

HUMAN LIFE, then, is not of man's manufacture; on the contrary, life derives from God who freely bestows it both as *Creator* — he summons life from nothingness — and as *Father* — the life he gives man is given in love, to persons he views as his children.

THE INSTRUCTION goes on to acknowledge advances made in the biological and medical sciences, by means of which ever more effective therapeutic resources have been acquired. At the same time, however, these sciences have opened up new powers "with unforeseeable consequences" over human life, both at its beginning and within its first stages. Thus, the processes of procreation can now not only be assisted in new ways, but actually dominated. Moreover, the temptation is present to go beyond "a reasonable dominion over nature," as Pope John Paul II remarked to a convention of Italian physicians and surgeons on 27 October 1980. (Ibid., footnote No. 1)

THIS TEMPTATION has been analyzed by solid thinkers such as Dr. Raymond Dennehy, professor of philosophy at the University of San Francisco. Discussing it in terms of the ancient Myth of Prometheus, who, in one version, stole fire from the gods, and in another, created man, Dr. Dennehy has argued: ". . . the *elan* of post-Christian Prometheanism warns us that man's ontological reach extends beyond his ontological grasp. It induces in man a *forgetfulness of his creaturehood and intrinsic limitation.* Secular humanism's failure to see that creaturehood is not a condition that can be overcome blinds its apostles to the insuperable obstacles in their path." (See "The Biological Revolution and the Myth of Prometheus," in *Pope John Paul II Lecture Series in Bioethics*, Vol. II, ed. Francis J. Lescoe and David Q. Liptak, Cromwell, 1986, p. 11; italics added)

TO BE a creature, therefore, is not to be a being who finally rules and measures; God alone rules and measures. To be a creature is to be one who "is ruled and measured." For the creature there are some aspirations which cannot be achieved; indeed, they ought not to be attempted. (Ibid., p. 26)

THAT MODERN SCIENCE and technology are widely perceived as having crossed the threshold of reasonable exploration and/or experimentation with respect to human technological reproduction is evident from the fact that, as the Instruction notes, "many people are . . . expressing an urgent appeal that in interventions on procreation the values and rights of the human person be safeguarded." Moreover, requests "for clarification and guidance are coming not only from the faithful but also from those who recognize the Church as 'an expert in humanity' with a mission to serve the 'civilization of love' and life." (Introduction, Sec. 1)

OF COURSE, the Church does not intervene in science or technology on the basis of a particular expertise in the area of these disciplines; the Church's competence here is bedrock to that relating to any honest human endeavor; namely, that of applying solid and perennial moral criteria. These criteria are 1) the respect, defense and advancement of each and every human person; 2) his or her primary and fundamental right to life; 3) his or her dignity as a person endowed with a spiritual soul with a moral responsibility and 4) the truth that all persons are called to beatific communion with God. (Ibid.)

FURTHERMORE, the Church is prompted to speak out on technological reproduction from a sense of love it owes to mankind, a love which impels it to help mankind recognize and respect rights and responsibilities; a love drawn from the fount of Jesus' love for mankind. (Ibid.)

SCIENCE and technology, after all, are not to be viewed as ultimate disciplines, free from the basic moral norms which direct and give meaning to all human acts without exception; nor are science and technology their own ethical arbiters. Rather, these disciplines are both ordered to mankind, and lie at the service of mankind. Hence "they draw from the person and his moral values the indication of their purpose and the awareness of their limits." (Ibid., Sec. 2)

IN OTHER WORDS, it is unreasonable to hold that science and technology are ethically neutral pursuits; nor can ethical norms be derived simply from their utilitarian or apparently efficient implementation. Realistically, both require, for their own intrinsic meaning, "an unconditional respect for the fundamental criteria of the moral law." Which is to restate that they must always be at the service of the human person, of his or her inalienable rights, and of his or her true and integral good according to God's will." (Ibid.)

Procreation, Not Reproduction

Since the human person cannot be reduced simply to a complex of tissue but must be seen as a composite of body and soul — spirit expressed by body — human sexuality cannot be equated with that found in the animal world. This principle obviously must be respected with regard to the beginning of human life.

In the human being, sexuality goes to the very depths of the person. Sexual communion is an interpersonal act, reflecting the love of God, Creator and Father. As such, sexual communion is ordained to take place within marriage, which possesses specific goods and values in its union and in procreation, which cannot be likened to those existing in lower forms of life.

TWO FUNDAMENTAL values are therefore apposite to this discussion, as the Instruction on the gift of life and the sanctity of procreation emphasizes. One is the life of the human being called into existence: *each human being, from the moment of conception, is unique, precious and unrepeatable.* The second is the special nature of the transmission of human life in marriage: *an act of procreation, not simply of reproduction.*

AS FOR the first, the "inviolability of the innocent human being's right to life 'from the moment of conception until death' is," the Instruction argues, "a sign and a requirement of the very inviolability of the person to whom the Creator has given the gift of life." (Introduction, Sec. 4) Whereas physical life does not itself contain the whole of a person's value, and whereas it does not "represent the supreme good of man who is called to eternal life," nonetheless it does constitute in a certain manner the "fundamental" value of life, precisely because upon this physical life all the other values of the person are based and developed. (Ibid.)

AS FOR the second value, that of transmission of human life, it must be acknowledged that this is invested with a special character which derives from the precious nature of the human person. As Pope John XXIII explained in his encyclical *Mater et Magistra* (1961): "The transmission of human life is entrusted by nature to a personal and conscious act and as such is subject to the all-holy laws of God: immutable and inviolable laws which must be recognized and observed. For this reason, one cannot use means and follow methods which could be licit in the transmission of the life of plants and animals." (Section III)

MODERN TECHNOLOGY, the Instruction grants, has made possible the initiation of human life outside of sexual relations by, for example, the union of gametes in a laboratory situation. That this is technically possible, however, does not mean that it is ethically admissible. Ethical admissibility depends on rational reflection of the fundamental values of life and of procreation.

SUCH RATIONAL reflection is aided by the light of divine Revelation, which the Magisterium — the teaching authority — of the Church provides. Under such illumination, man is reminded of such truths as these: 1) the life of each and every human being should be respected in an absolute way because man is the only creature whom God has "wished for himself" (See Vatican Council II, the Pastoral Constitution on the

Church in the Modern World, n. 24); 2) the spiritual soul of each person is immediately created by God (See the encyclical *Humani Generis*, Pope Pius XII, 1950; Section 42); 3) man's whole being bears the image of God the Creator (Ibid.); 4) Human life is sacred from its conception because it involves the creative action of God (See Pope John Paul II, "Responsible Procreation," 17 September 1983: "At the origin of each human person there is a creative act of God; no man comes into existence by chance; he is always the result of the creative love of God."); 5) human life remains forever in special relationship with God the Creator who is its only goal (See Pastoral Constitution on the Church in the Modern World, n. 24); God and only God is the Lord of life from its origin to its close; hence no one can claim for himself or herself the right to destroy or interdict directly an innocent human being. (See Pope Pius XII, Discourse to the St. Luke Medical-Biological Union, 12 November 1944)

AS REGARDS the second "value," these truths are set forth clearly by the Magisterium: 1) human procreation requires, on the part of the spouses, responsible collaboration with the fruitful love of God, our Creator and Father (Pastoral Constitution on the Church in the Modern World, n. 50); the gift of human life must be actualized in marriage through the specific and exclusive acts of spouses, in accordance with the laws inscribed into their persons and in their union. (Ibid., n. 51)

Experimenting In General

Part I of the Vatican Instruction on the gift of life and the holiness of procreation treats six questions on the topic, "Respect for human embryos." In sequence these are: 1) What respect is due to the human embryo, taking into account his nature and identity? 2) Is prenatal diagnosis morally licit? 3) Are therapeutic procedures carried out on the human embryo licit? 4) How is one morally to evaluate research and experimentation on human embryos and fetuses? 5) How is one to evaluate morally the use for research purposes of embryos obtained by fertilization "in vitro"? and 6) What judgment should be made on other procedures of manipulating embryos connected with the "techniques of human reproduction"?

THE FIRST QUESTION is fundamental. What respect is due to the human embryo, given his — note that word *his*, not *its* — nature and identity?

THE ONLY response possible in the light of Christian doctrine — the Bible and Tradition conveyed by the Church's Magisterium; reason illumined by Revelation — is that *the human being must be* viewed always as a *person*, from the very *first instant of his existence.* (Instruction I:1)

AS REGARDS any kind of experimentation, therefore — and this is the first problem that arises in the context of scientific or technological endeavor — a cardinal principle to be acknowledged is that "human life must be absolutely respected and protected from the moment of conception." (See the Vatican's *Charter of the Rights of the Family*, Section 4, in *L'Osservatore Romano*, 25 November 1983)

THUS the Church's constant position is that the child conceived must be respected *from the moment of conception*. As the Vatican Document on Procured Abortion puts it:

"FROM THE TIME that the ovum is fertilized, a new life is begun which is neither that of the father nor of the mother; it is rather the life of a new human being with his own growth. It would never be made human if it were not human already. To this perpetual evidence modern genetic science brings valuable confirmation. It has demonstrated that, from the first instant, the program is fixed as to what this living being will be: a man, this individual man with his characteristic aspects already well determined. Right from fertilization is begun the adventure of a human life, and each of its great capacities requires time . . . to find its place and to be in a position to act." (Congregation for the Doctrine of the Faith, 1974; Sections 12-13.)

This doctrine is clearly confirmed — were confirmation needed — by recent findings in human biology; data acknowledge that in the zygote resulting from fertilization, the biological identity of a new human individual is already established. Hence in the zygote we are *not* speaking of *potential* human life, but of *actual* human life.

What about the soul? Must we await the collection of experimental data prior to our maintaining unreservedly the soul's existence from the moment of conception? Here the Instruction puts another question: namely, "How could a human individual not be a human person?"

Although the Instruction does not digress here with philosophical data, the Thomistic doctrine — the doctrine reasoned out by St. Thomas Aquinas — does not allow for body and soul as clearly separable entities.

Since man is a composite of body and soul, there is only one act of creation, that of the soul, which receives the body in the communion of its own being. Etienne Gilson, one of the modern world's most respected interpreters of Aquinas, wrote:

"The soul . . . has the being of a substance, and nevertheless it shares its being with the body; more precisely, it receives the body in the communion of its own act of being . . . Were it not so, the whole being of man would not be one, and the unity of man would not be a substantial unity . . . there is only one act of being, that of the soul, for the whole individual human substance, including the form, the matter and all the individuation . . ." (*The Elements of Christian Philosophy*, Doubleday, 1960, pp. 228-9.)

On the basis of the aforesaid, traditional ethical principles relating to experimentation obtain, the first of which is (as ethicist Paul Ramsey describes it) "the canon of loyalty"; namely, that experimentation on a human being always requires his or her consent (See *Human Existence, Medicine and Ethics* by William E. May, 1977.) This "canon of loyalty" literally opens the famed Nuremberg Code, composed in the context of Nazi atrocities perpetrated against human beings: "The voluntary consent of the human subject is absolutely essential." The Ethical and Religious Directives for Catholic Health Facilities, No. 27, puts it this way: "Experimentation on patients without due consent is morally objectionable, and even the moral right of a patient to consent is limited by his duties of stewardship."

Experimentation can be 1) therapeutic (e.g., healing, medicinal), 2) nontherapeutic (e.g., for research) and 3) mixed or borderline (e.g., to advance knowledge and benefit the subject.) Free and informed consent must be honored in all human experimentation, therapeutic or nontherapeutic.

Experimentation upon the unborn child — in any stage following its conception — is ruled by the same moral principles that apply to a person. Since the unborn child cannot give his or her own consent, what ethical norms determine proxy consent in this regard? As far as therapeutic experimentation goes, such consent is generally justified; e.g., parents' consenting for the child in need of help. But what about nontherapeutic experimentation?

The answer here is in the negative precisely because, in Dr. William May's words, such a procedure "strikes at the heart of the belief or presupposition that makes the principle of free and informed consent intelligible and true to begin with; namely, that all human beings, simply by reason of their membership in the human species, are beings of moral worth and, as such, entities that transcend the communities in which they live." (op. cit.)

Hence children within the womb cannot be "volunteered" for experiments in which they, because of their condition, cannot be true volunteers.

Therapeutic Experimentation (Prenatal Testing)

Resting its responses on the traditional principles regarding human experimentation, *especially the norm that any experimentation requires informed consent*, Part I of the Vatican Instruction on the gift of life and the holiness of procreation asks four specific questions. First, is prenatal diagnosis morally permissible? Secondly, are therapeutic procedures upon the human embryo licit? Thirdly, how can one morally assess research upon embryos obtained by *in vitro* fertilization? Lastly, what judgment should be made regarding other procedures of manipulating embryos connected with so-called "techniques of human reproduction"?

AS TO the first, that of prenatal diagnosis, the Instruction states that if it respects the life and integrity of the embryo or the fetus, and is directed toward safeguarding or healing the embryo or fetus, then it is morally licit.

THE ISSUE, in this case, is investigation oriented toward therapeutic intervention. The necessary consent can be given by the parents, once they have been adequately informed. The words "respects," "safeguarding" and "healing" imply of course that disproportionate risk is not involved.

What, however, if a prenatal diagnosis is done with the thought of possibly inducing an abortion, if the results indicate some abnormality? In this case, the procedure — amniocentesis, say — would be gravely opposed to the moral law. A diagnosis indicating fetal malformation or hereditary illness, "must not be the equivalent of a death sentence." (Instruction, I:2)

THE VATICAN Instruction spells out this response: "Thus a woman would be committing a gravely illicit act if she were to request such a diagnosis with the deliberate intention of having an abortion, should the result confirm the existence of a malformation or abnormality. The spouse or relatives or anyone else would similarly be acting in a manner contrary to the moral law if they were to counsel or impose such a diagnostic procedure on the expectant mother with the same intention . . . So too the specialist would be guilty of illicit collaboration if, in conducting the diagnosis, and in communicating its results, he were deliberately to contribute to establishing or forming a link between prenatal diagnosis and abortion." (Ibid.)

HERE the Instruction adds that any attempt by civil or health authorities to link prenatal diagnosis with abortion is to be condemned *as a violation of the unborn child's right to life and as an abuse of the prior rights and duties of the spouses.*

SECONDLY, are therapeutic procedures on the embryo morally allowable?

IN RESPONSE, the Instruction recalls the words of John Paul II to participants in the 35th General Assembly of the World Medical Association on 23 October 1983:

"A STRICTLY therapeutic intervention whose explicit objective is the healing of various maladies such as those stemming from chromosomal defects will, in principle, be considered desirable, provided it is directed to the true promotion of the personal well-being of the individual without doing harm to his integrity or worsening his conditions of life. Such an intervention would indeed fall within the logic of the Christian moral tradition." (Ibid. I:3)

THUS, *since the embryo is a person*, the principle of therapeutic intervention regarding persons *applies as well to human life at its beginning.* As the Instruction puts it: ". . . One must uphold as licit procedures which respect the life and integrity of the embryo and do not involve disproportionate risks for it that are directed toward its healing, the improvement of its condition of health, or its individual survival." (Ibid.)

THIRDLY, what about *experimentation* upon human embryos or fetuses? *Experimentation* means any research in which the human being — in various states of existence — represents the object through which or upon which one intends to verify the effect, at present unknown or not adequately known, of a given treatment; e.g., surgical, pharmacological. (Ibid., footnote No. 28)

THE ONLY moral response to this question of *experimentation* upon human embryos and fetuses has to be in the *negative.* As John Paul II explained to a meeting of the Pontifical Academy of Sciences on 23 October 1982: "I condemn, in the most explicit and formal way, experimental manipulations of the human embryo, since the human being, from conception to death, cannot be exploited for any purpose whatever." (Ibid., Footnote No. 29)

MORE ABOUT THIS in the next chapter. Here, however, one could point out that the Instruction draws a distinction between experimentation and research. "Research" means any inductive-deductive process which aims at promoting the systematic observation of a given phenomenon in the human field or at verifying a hypothesis arising from previous observations. (Ibid. Footnote 26:1). The norm to be followed in this regard is: Medical research must refrain from operations on live embryos unless there is a moral certainty of not causing harm to the life or integrity of the unborn child and the mother, and on condition that the parents have given their free and informed consent to the procedure." (Ibid. I:4)

IT FOLLOWS that research, even when limited to the simple observation of the embryo, would be morally inadmissible were it to entail risk to the embryo's physical integrity, or life, because of the methods employed or the effects induced.

Nontherapeutic Experimentation

Nontherapeutic experimentation on human embryos or fetuses is assessed ethically in Part I, No. 4 of the Vatican Instruction on the gift of life and the holiness of procreation.

THE CHARTER of Rights of the Family, issued by Pope John Paul II on 25 November 1982, reads in part: "Respect for the dignity of the human being excludes all experimental manipulation or exploitation of the human embryo." (Section 4b)

WHAT IS under discussion here is experimentation that is *not directly therapeutic.* The question at issue, as put by the Instruction, reads: "How is one to evaluate morally . . . experimentation on human embryos or fetuses?" (Instruction I:4)

THE INSTRUCTION draws a distinction between experimentation on live embryos, and embryos which are not alive. If embryos are living, they must be treated as living human beings. Whether viable or not, they must be "respected just like any human person." (Ibid.) Hence, experimentation on embryos that is not directly therapeutic is morally inadmissible.

COULD THIS moral judgment bend to the verification of so-called "noble goals" for experimentation? For example, could the acquisition of new scientific data justify each experimentation? Or alleged potential benefit to society?

THE INSTRUCTION'S answer is one already reflected in the principles outlined in its Introduction. Thus, it states, unequivocally and firmly: "No objective, even though noble in itself, such as a foreseeable advantage to science, to other human beings or to society, can in any way justify experimentation on living human embryos or fetuses, whether viable or not, either inside or outside the mother's womb."

THE MORAL ISSUE here transcends the problem of who can give consent — the parents, say, or another responsible adult. Rather, it is that proxy consent cannot be ethically given here — as I pointed out in early chapters of this commentary. Again, a cardinal principle regarding validity of proxy consent for experimentation is that such experimentation must be *therapeutic* — directed toward the healing or betterment of the person on whom experimentation is to be done.

IN THE Instruction's words: "The informed consent ordinarily required for clinical experimentation on adults cannot be granted by the parents, *who may not fully dispose* of the physical integrity or life of the unborn child." (Ibid.)

MOREOVER, there is the risk factor. Experimentation on embryos and fetuses always entails risks; in most cases, the "certain expectation of harm to their physical integrity or even their death." (Ibid.)

THUS the moral judgment in summary is this: "To use human embryos or fetuses as the object or instrument of experimentation *constitutes a crime against their dignity as human beings having a right to the same respect that is due to the child already born and to every human person.*" (Ibid., Italics added.)

ONE VERY SPECIFIC problem in this context pertains to the use of drugs or procedures not yet fully tested, but potentially helpful. What about using these in extreme cases where the life of the embryo or fetus is threatened? Assuming that 1) the experimentation is clearly therapeutic; 2) the therapy is oriented toward the benefit of the embryo or fetus in a final effort to save the unborn's life; and 3) all other reliable forms of therapy are wanting; then "recourse to drugs or procedures not yet fully tested, can be licit." (Ibid.) Obviously each case must be evaluated individually or at least in terms of authentic medical-ethical norms.

THIS PRINCIPLE was stated earlier by the Congregation for the Doctrine of the Faith in 1980, in its important Declaration on Euthanasia: "In the absence of other sufficient remedies, it is permitted, with the patient's consent, to have recourse to the means provided by the most advanced medical techniques, even if these means are still at the experimental stage and are not without a certain risk." (AAS 72 [1980] 550)

FINALLY the question of experimentation on lifeless embryos or fetuses must be addressed. Is this ethically allowable? The Instruction sounds a strong negative reply, regardless of whether the embryos or fetuses have been deliberately aborted or not. On the contrary, they must be respected just as the mortal remains of other human beings are.

THE INSTRUCTION adds that lifeless embryos or fetuses cannot morally be subjected to mutilation or autopsy if their death has not been verified, and without the consent of the mother or the parents. Further, all moral norms must be observed to avoid complicity in deliberate abortion, and lest scandal be given. Lastly, all commercial trafficking with respect to lifeless embryos or fetuses is morally wrong and should be prohibited.

For a recent discussion of some of the problems cited above, see Dr. Donald De Marco's *Infertility and "In Vitro" Fertilization, Its Meaning and Morality* (Saskatchewan, 1985).

'Freezing' and Manipulating Embryos

Part I of the Vatican Instruction on the gift of life and the sanctity of procreation ends with these two questions: "How is one to evaluate morally the use for research purposes of embryos obtained by fertilization *in vitro*?" and "What judgment should be made on other procedures of manipulating embryos connected with the 'techniques of human reproduction'?"

As to the first, the point is strongly made that embryos obtained *in vitro* — so-called test-tube embryos, originating from the union of gametes in a petri dish — *are human beings* and, accordingly, are *subjects with rights*. Their dignity and right to life must be respected from the first instant of their existence.

TO PRODUCE human embryos destined for exploitation as disposable "biological material" is therefore *immoral*. (Instruction I:5).

HERE the instruction takes note of what is commonly called "wastage." As *in vitro* is usually carried out, not all the embryos are transferred from the petri dish to a woman's body; some are destroyed — literally wasted.

THE SPECIFIC immorality of such wastage is equivalent to abortion. As the Church condemns induced abortion, so the Church condemns interdicting the lives of these embryos.

THE VATICAN Instruction sees the researcher who resorts to such wastage as usurping the place of God.

Although he may not be aware of it, he sets himself up as the master of the destiny of others, inasmuch as he arbitrarily chooses whom he will permit to go on living, and whom he will consign to death; and he goes on to take the lives of defenseless innocents.

THUS, the Instruction warns: "*It is a duty to condemn the particular gravity of the voluntary destruction of human embryos obtained 'in vitro'* for the sole purpose of research, either by means of artificial insemination or by means of 'twin fission.'" (Ibid.)

FOR THE SAME reasons cited above, methods of observation or experimentation that damage embryos, or that impose grave and disproportionately heavy risks upon embryos obtained *in vitro*, are also morally illicit. Again, embryos are human beings, and human beings must be respected for themselves; they cannot be reduced in worth to mere instruments for others' advantage. Hence, the Instruction states, *"it is . . . not in conformity with the moral law deliberately to expose to death human embryos obtained 'in vitro.'"* (Ibid.)

THE LAST question of Part I of the Vatican Instruction discusses "other forms" of genetic or biological manipulation to which human embryos brought into existence by technological reproduction are subjected in theory or in fact. Among these are 1) attempts or plans for fertilization between human and animal gametes in animal uteruses; 2) the hypothesis of constructing artificial wombs for human embryos in technological reproduction.

SUCH PROCEDURES, declares the Instruction, *"are contrary to the human dignity proper to the embryo, and at the same time they are contrary to the right of every person to be conceived and to be born within marriage and from marriage."* (Ibid., I, 6)

(OF COURSE no one can demand a subjective right *to begin to exist*. However it is proper to assert the right of a child to have a fully human origin through conception in conformity with the personal nature of human beings. Life, a gift, must be bestowed in a way worthy of both the subject who receives it, and the subjects procreating it.)

AS FOR hypotheses for obtaining human beings through "twin fission," cloning, or parthenogenesis, these are also *"contrary to the moral law since they are in opposition to the dignity both of human procreation and of the conjugal union."* (Ibid.)

WHAT ABOUT freezing embryos — so-called cryopreservation? Even when done allegedly "to preserve the life of an embryo," such manipulation *"constitutes an offense against the respect due to human beings."* (Ibid.)

BY THIS process, the embryos are subjected to grave risks of death or harm to their physical integrity; too, they are thereby deprived, at least for the time, of maternal shelter and/or gestation, and, by this situation, made vulnerable to further manipulation.

FINALLY, Part I of the Instruction concludes, certain attempts *"to influence chromosomic or genetic inheritance are not therapeutic but are aimed at producing human beings selected according to sex or other predetermined qualities. These manipulations are contrary to the personal dignity of the human being and his or her integrity or identity."* (Ibid.) Thus they cannot be justified on the basis of possible benefits for humanity. Every person must be respected in himself or herself, from the very beginning.

Artificial Forms

Part II of the Instruction on the gift of life and the holiness of human procreation is entitled, "Interventions upon Human Procreation." It begins with an explanation of terms or phrases.

First, "artificial procreation" and "artificial fertilization" are described as those various technical procedures intended toward obtaining human conception in a manner other than the sexual union of man and woman. This is what is generally described as "technological reproduction." It includes *in vitro* fertilization, referred to as "test tube" conception, and artificial insemination.

THE FIRST, *in vitro* fertilization, is often cited by the abbreviation IVF; artificial insemination is called AI. When artificial insemination occurs through transfer of sperm from the subject's (woman's) husband, it is called AIH; when the sperm is that of a man other than the subject's husband, it is called AID (Artificial Insemination, Donor) or AIV (Artificial Insemination, Vendor). I often prefer the adjective "Vendor," since this process is usually a commercial transaction, whereas "donor" implies a gift. "Vector is another word used for "V." (See Glossary of Terms)

A THIRD FORM of technological reproduction is also cited here; namely, Embryo Transfer, abbreviated as ET. ET can begin with IVF or AI.

THE VATICAN Instruction uses the phrases "heterologous artificial fertilization" and "homologous artificial fertilization." (Instruction, A1 and B1) By "heterologous artificial fertilization" is meant "techniques used to obtain a human conception artificially by the use of gametes coming from at least one donor other than the spouses . . . joined in marriage." (Ibid., Note No. 33)

THESE TECHNIQUES can be of two varieties: 1) heterologous IVF and ET ("the technique . . . to obtain a human conception through the meeting *in vitro* of gametes taken from at least one donor other than the two spouses joined in marriage"; and 2) heterologous artificial insemination ("the technique used to obtain a human conception through the genital tracts of the woman . . . [with] sperm previously collected from a donor other than the husband." (Ibid.)

BY "artificial homologous fertilization" the Instruction means "the technique used to obtain a human conception using the gametes of the two spouses joined in marriage." This technique can be implemented in two ways: 1) homologous IVF and ET ("used to obtain a human conception through the meeting *in vitro* of the gametes of the spouses joined in marriage") and 2) homologous artificial insemination ("used to obtain a human conception through the transfer into the genital tracts of a married woman of the sperm previously collected from her husband." (Ibid.)

SO THAT the Vatican's categories differ from the standard categories employed in medical usage here.

THE VATICAN Instruction, to recapitulate, refers to technological reproduction in general as "artificial fertilization." It then goes on to distinguish artificial fertilization into two categories: "heterologous" (where the gametes are from at least one "donor" other than the spouse) and "homologous" (where the gametes involved are from the spouses, not from a third party). Further, each of these categories includes two methodologies: 1) IVF and/or ET (*in vitro* fertilization and embryo transfer) and 2) AI (artificial insemination).

HAVING OFFERED these definitions and distinctions, the Instruction asks a series of questions. The first is crucial and must be answered before any of the others; namely, why must human procreation take place in marriage?

THE PROCREATION of a new person, the Instruction reminds, whereby marrieds collaborate with the power of the Creator, must be "the fruit and the sign of the mutual self-giving of the spouses, of their love and of their fidelity. *The fidelity of the spouses in the unity of marriage involves reciprocal respect of their right to become a father and a mother only through each other.*" (Ibid., II, 1)

ACTUALLY a child has a right to be conceived, borne in the womb, brought into the world and brought up within marriage. It is "through the secure and recognized relationship to his own parents that the child can discover his own identity and achieve his proper human development." (Ibid.)

MOREOVER, parents discover in their child "a confirmation and completion of their reciprocal self-giving: the child is the living image of their love, the permanent sign of their conjugal union, the living and indissoluble concrete expression of their paternity and maternity." (Ibid.)

FURTHER, by reason of the vocation and social responsibility of the person, the good of children and parents enhances the good of civil society. The stability and vitality of society require that children come into the world within a family, and that this family be solidly founded upon marriage. Marriage and its indissoluble unity is the only context worthy of truly responsible procreation.

Heterologous Conception

Heterologous artificial fertilization is discussed in Part II, Section A, No. 1 of the Vatican Instruction on the gift of life and the holiness of procreation. At issue here are 1) artificial insemination by donor or vendor (AID or AIV); 2) *in vitro* fertilization entailing the use of a gamete from a third party (IVF); and 3) embryo transfer entailing use of a gamete from a third party (ET).

Is such fertilization, in which the gamete of a third party is employed, in conformity with 1) the dignity of the couple who opt for it; and 2) the truth of marriage?

THE ANSWER is of course flatly in the negative. *"Heterologous artificial fertilization,"* the Instruction teaches, *"is contrary to the unity of marriage, to the dignity of the spouses, to the vocation proper to parents, and to the child's right to be conceived and brought into the world in marriage and from marriage."* (Instruction, A2)

THUS, AID (AIV), IVF and ET using a third party's gametes are judged inconsonant with the dignity of marriage.

RESPECT FOR the unity of marriage (e.g., this wife is the *only* partner for this husband, and he is the *only* spouse for her) and for conjugal fidelity (each partner's loyalty to the other, to the exclusion of any other partner, by virtue of their marriage vows), *demands that a child be conceived within marriage.*

INDEED, the right to become father and mother of a child must be realized exclusively through each other —

husband and wife. Recourse to the gametes of a third person, in the form of either sperm or ovum — violates the reciprocal commitment of the spouses and constitutes a serious deficiency with respect to the unity of marriage, one of its essential properties.

FURTHERMORE, AID (donor or vendor insemination) and IVF or ET using donor or vendor sperm or ova, are judged violations of the rights of the child. Each deprives the child of his or her filial relationship with his or her parental origins and can retard the maturing of his personal identity.

FURTHER STILL, such technological reproduction insults the common vocation of spouses called to fatherhood and motherhood. Thus, it effects a rupture between genetic parenthood and parental responsibility for upbringing. This in turn has grave consequences with respect to society, since the family is the basic unit of society. Whatever assails the unity and stability of the family, adversely impacts the whole of social life.

FOR ALL these reasons, the Instruction concludes, *"fertilization of a married woman with the sperm of a donor different from her husband and fertilization with the husband's sperm of an ovum not coming from his wife are morally illicit. Furthermore, the artificial fertilization of a woman who is unmarried or a widow, whoever the donor may be, cannot be morally justified.*

HERE the Instruction adds that the desire on the part of spouses to have a child despite sterility is understandable, but subjectively good intentions cannot alter the morality of procedures in themselves wrong. Besides, children are to be viewed as gifts — benedictions from

God. Strictly speaking, no spouses have a right to children.

SEVERAL BIBLICAL texts witness to this principle: Genesis 4:1, Genesis 4:25; First Samuel 1:27, etc. The first text is Eve's exclamation, following the birth of Cain: "I have produced a man with the help of God." The second is also Eve's word; this time it follows Seth's birth: "God has granted me more offspring in place of Abel." And the last is Hanna's prayer of thanksgiving, when Samuel was given her: "I prayed for this child, and the Lord granted my request."

MARRIEDS who falsely view children as a right can readily argue that this right entails another one, that of having children by whatever means including any artificial procedures that modern technology can offer (e.g., AIH, AID, IVF, surrogate parenting, etc.).

"Surrogate" Motherhood

Section 3 of Part II, A, of the Vatican Instruction on the gift of life and the sanctity of procreation cites surrogate motherhood, specifically; is "surrogate" motherhood morally permissible?

The answer is in the negative, for the same reasons that render heterologous artificial fertilization (e.g., AID, IVF) ethically unacceptable. In other words, surrogate motherhood is contrary to the unity of marriage and to the dignity of procreation.

AS THE Instruction puts it: "Surrogate motherhood represents an objective failure to meet the obligations of maternal love, of conjugal fidelity and of responsible motherhood; it offends the dignity and the right of the child to be conceived, carried in the womb, brought into the world and brought up by his own parents; it sets up, to the detriment of families, a division between the physical, psychological and moral elements which constitute those families." (Instruction, II, A3)

"SURROGATE" motherhood generally describes a woman's allowing her ova and/or womb for the conception, gestation and birth of a child whom she has agreed to bear for a couple; the child is destined to be handed over to the couple with whom the biological mother has contracted.

MANY KINDS of surrogate motherhood are possible. One makes use of artificial insemination (AID or AIV) with the sperm of the contracting father; another, embryonic transfer, after a child is first conceived *in vitro*. Another form is surrogate embryo transfer (SET) which entails artificial insemination of a woman, with removal of the embryo at an early stage of development (fifth to seventh day) by intrauterine flushing; the embryo is then transferred to the uterine cavity of the female who will carry the fetus to term and eventual delivery. (For the above medical data, I am relying on the Glossary of Terms and lecture notes prepared by Leo T. Duffy, M.D., who wrote the second part of this book, wherein the Glossary appears in full.)

THE VATICAN Instruction's meaning of "surrogate mother" extends to all the various modalities. Hence, "surrogate mother" refers to 1) a woman who carries in pregnancy an embryo implanted in her uterus and who is genetically a stranger to the embryo because it has been obtained through the union of the gametes of "donors"; she carries the pregnancy with the pledge to give up the baby once the child is born to the party with whom she contracted; and 2) a woman who carries in pregnancy an embryo to whose procreation she has contributed the donation of her own ovum, fertilized by means of insemination with the sperm of a man other than her husband; she carries the child with a pledge to surrender him or her following birth to the party who commissioned or made the agreement for the pregnancy. (Note No. 37, II, A3)

IN 1984, ethicist Father Albert S. Moraczewski of the Pope John XXIII Medical-Moral Center (now located in Braintree, Mass.) observed that there are "Twelve ways to Make a Baby." The number "12" was calculated by combining, in various ways, different sources of ova or sperm, and the various possibilities of surrogate motherhood. Thus, the sperm can be taken from the husband, or from a donor (vendor, vector); the ovum, from the wife of the "surrogate" spouse or from a donor; and the embryo can be carried within the womb of either the donor or the woman who desires the child, or even a third-party mother. Then there are variations of embryonic transfer, including the possibility of conceiving and carrying an embryo not until term, but only until "transfer time" to a woman who wants to be called the surrogate mother. (This is sometimes called "interuterine adoption" to distinguish it from ordinary surrogate motherhood.) (Ethics and Medics, issue of December 1984)

INCIDENTALLY, surrogate motherhood can be distinguished from surrogate gestation. As Bishop Walter W. Curtis of Bridgeport once put it (in what is an excellent summary of the subject):

"QUITE DIFFERENT . . . is 'surrogate gestation,' in which a child conceived by its proper parents is transplanted to the womb of another woman when its own mother for serious reasons of health cannot continue the pregnancy until the viability of the child.

"FOR SERIOUS reasons of health of mother or child such 'surrogate gestation' could be permitted morally. Whether this procedure will ever be necessary is left to the judgment of the doctors." (The Catholic Transcript, 13 April 1984)

Homologous Fertilization

Heterologous artificial fertilization — technological reproduction that utilizes the gametes of a third party, regardless of the mode (e.g., artificial insemination, *in vitro* fertilization) is found morally deficient in Section A of Part II of the Instruction on the gift of life and the sacredness of procreation.

WHAT, however, about homologous artificial fertilization? In other words: is artificial fertilization morally allowable if the gametes (sperm, ova) utilized are exclusively those of the spouses who desire to have a child? Husband and wife: can they morally resort to technological reproduction if they have no other way of having a family?

GRANTED, such artificial fertilization does not raise the moral problem of adultery or fornication, since only the spouses are involved. But there are more fundamental moral objections.

FOR ONE THING, AIH (artificial insemination by husband) or IVF (using the gametes of the spouses) or ET (embryonic transfer from, say, a petri dish) reduces the generation of a child as a person to the production of a child as an object. This violates the fundamental ethical norm that (as theologian William E. May puts it) children are meant to be "begotten, not made." (*Perspectives in Bioethics*, Vol. I, Mariel Publications, 1983, p. 55)

THE VATICAN Instruction explains: "In his unique and irreplaceable origin, the child must be respected and recognized as equal in personal dignity to those who give him life. The human person must be accepted in his parents' act of union and love; the generation of a child must therefore be the fruit of that mutual giving which is realized in the conjugal act wherein the spouses cooperate as servants and not as masters in the work of the Creator who is Love . . .

". . . A HUMAN person . . . cannot be desired or conceived as the product of an intervention of medical or biological techniques; that would be equivalent to reducing him to an object of scientific technology. No one may subject the coming of a child into the world to conditions of technological efficiency which are to be evaluated according to standards of control and dominion." (Instruction, II, B4)

FURTHERMORE, artificial fertilization separates the love-giving (unitive) meaning of conjugal communion from the life-giving (procreative) meaning.

CONJUGAL communion is not simply a union of bodies, much less of gametes. On the contrary, it is an *interpersonal* union, one which involves body and spirit. Spouses mutually express their personal love through the "language of the body" which clearly manifests spousal *and* parental meanings. Conjugal communion is inseparably spiritual as well as corporal. One cannot separate the life-giving meaning from the love-giving meaning without making conjugal communion something the Creator never intended it to be; indeed, it is a contradiction of the innate language of conjugal union.

IN THE words of the Instruction: "Homologous artificial fertilization, in seeking a procreation which is not the fruit of a specific act of conjugal union, objectively effects an analogous separation between the goods and the meanings of marriage." (Ibid.)

THE DOCTRINE spelling out the reasons why the procreative meaning of conjugal union cannot be separated from the creative meaning, is precisely stated in Pope Paul VI's encyclical *Humanae Vitae* and Pope John Paul II's Apostolic Exhortation, *Familiaris Consortio*. The new (1983) Code of Canon Law summarizes this doctrine in Canon 1061, which stresses that the conjugal act is that act by which marriage is consummated if the couple have performed it between themselves in a human manner.

IT MAKES no difference what form of artificial fertilization is employed: AIH, IVF, ET. Any kind of technological reproduction is contraindicated by moral norms.

IT IS TRUE, of course, that homologous fertilization is not characterized by the ethical negativity found in extra-conjugal, technological reproduction (e.g., AID, IVF utilizing the gametes of a third party). Here marriage and the family continue to constitute the environment for the birth and upbringing of children. Nonetheless, the procedure is still immoral; it is depersonalizing both to the child and to the couple.

FURTHER, even in homologous fertilization, there is the problem of wastage — the practice of destroying embryos, which is the moral equivalent of abortion, hence intrinsically evil.

ANOTHER ethical problem here pertains to one means by which sperm are collected; namely, masturbation. Such a technique is morally impermissible since it deprives human procreation of the dignity which is proper and natural to it — again, it separates the meanings of conjugal union.

THE VATICAN Instruction treats homologous artificial insemination (AIH) in a special section because it comments on a tangent issue; namely, whether technical means can be used not as a substitute for, but as an assist to, the natural purpose of conjugal communion. More about this in the next chapter.

ALSO, in the next chapter, a word about the love due to those who are born by means of artificial fertilization; though the method must be rejected, all persons must be accorded love.

Treating Sterility

Granted that artificial fertilization is morally objectionable, what about medical intervention in order *to assist* human procreation? In other words, can physicians and scientists morally intervene to facilitate the conception of new life through conjugal union?

This question is addressed in Part II, B, 7, of the Vatican Instruction on the gift of life and the sanctity of procreation.

MEDICINE must always be oriented toward the good of the person, not merely toward technical, scientific or utilitarian goals. This is to say that the ethics of medical practice must respect the integral goal of the person and the specifically human values of sexuality. Thus medical personnel are at the service of persons and of human *procreation*, which is sacred. (Again, I stress the word "procreation," as contradistinguished from "reproduction.")

DOES THIS MEAN that medical or scientific personnel may not intervene in favor of human procreation? In the precise words of the Vatican Instruction: "A medical intervention respects the dignity of persons when it seeks to assist the conjugal act either in order to facilitate its performance or in order to enable it to achieve its objective once it has been normally performed." (Ibid.)

THIS does not mean that a medical procedure can technologically replace conjugal union in order to secure a "procreation" which is neither its result nor its fruit. In such an instance, the intervention is not at the service of conjugal union but instead appropriates to itself the procreative function and thus "contradicts the dignity and the inalienable rights of the spouses and of the child to be born." (Ibid.)

THEOLOGIAN Father Lorenzo M. Albacete summarizes this judgment in his Commentary on the Vatican Instruction on Bioethics, (St. Paul editions, 1987): "Biotechnological methods are permissible when they are not a substitute for the conjugal act, but intend to facilitate and help the act attain its natural purpose. They are meant to *assist* human procreation, not to *replace* it. This is part of the 'humanization of medicine' so needed today and in which Catholic health care personnel should play an exemplary part." (p. 20)

THIS LAST sentence reflects a strong reminder in the Vatican Instruction to Catholic hospitals, health care institutions and health care personnel (physicians, nurses, technicians, etc.) that the document should be observed as to its moral norms. Indeed, this reminder is made in the form of an "urgent appeal."

THE SUFFERINGS occasioned by sterility in marriage are discussed in the closing section of Part II, B (Section 8) of the Instruction.

WHATEVER ITS ORIGIN or prognosis, sterility is clearly a trial. "The community of believers," the Instruction declares, "is called to shed light upon and support the suffering of those who are unable to fulfill their legitimate aspiration to motherhood and fatherhood. Spouses who find themselves in this sad situation are called to find in it an opportunity for sharing in a particular way in the Lord's cross, the source of spiritual fruitfulness. Sterile couples must not forget that even when procreation is not possible, conjugal life does not for this reason lose its value. Physical sterility . . . can be for spouses the occasion for other important services to the life of the human person, for example adoption, various forms of education work, and assistance to other families and to poor or handicapped children." (Ibid.)

AGAIN, the Instruction cautions that spouses cannot look upon children as a right. Rather, a child is a gift from God, a benediction.

POPE PIUS XII explicitly affirmed this doctrine in an address to the Second World Congress on Fertility and Sterility, 20 May 1956. And Canon 1135 of the new (1983) Code of Canon Law stipulates that "each spouse has an equal obligation and right to whatever pertains to the partnership of conjugal life." But a right to have children is not stated. To say that such a right exists would offend against the imperatives arising from personalism, since such a right would be proximate to a right over other persons.

VIEWING offspring as the right of spouses supports the false argument that this alleged right entails another one; namely, that of having a child by whatever means technology can offer (e.g., AI, IVF, ET). It also leads to the false conclusion that spouses have a right to a healthy child. As moral theologians Donald G. McCarthy and Edward J. Bayer put it, this conclusion "leads to the further expectation that the child will be born perfect (without blemish of mind and body) by whatever standards are current. One consequence of such an attitude is that a child who is born less than perfect, or who has a defect or disorder, is likely to be rejected psychologically or even aborted." (*Critical Sexual Issues*, John XXIII Center, 1983)

A New Procedure

Part II of the Vatican Instruction on the gift of life and the holiness of procreation ends, as I have already noted, with a solid, highly sensitive, and helpful passage about the plight of spouses who, through no fault of their own, are not graced with children. The Instruction describes their situation as "a difficult trial."

"Many researchers," the Instruction goes on, "are engaged in the fight against sterility. While fully safeguarding the dignity of human procreation, some have achieved results which previously seemed unattainable. Scientists, therefore, are encouraged to continue their research with the aim of preventing the causes of sterility and of being able to remedy them so that sterile couples will be able to procreate in full respect for their own personal dignity and that of the child to be born." (Instruction II, B, 8)

PERHAPS an example of what is going on today to help couples will be helpful in this context; namely, "Low Tubal Ovum Transfer," known as LTOT.

LTOT IS a procedure designed to facilitate conception in certain cases of female infertility; specifically, when the wife suffers from damaged, blocked, diseased or absent Fallopian tubes. The key to this new procedure, developed by gynecologist David S. McLaughlin of Dayton, is retrieving the eggs through laparoscopy and promptly replacing them into the uterus or lower portion of the Fallopian tube.

THIS PROCEDURE is described in the October 1983 issue of Ethics and Medics, the newsletter published by the Pope John XXIII Center. In the article Father Donald G. McCarthy assesses LTOT as "a significant step in medical progress toward the authentic solution to infertility." Indeed, he notes that 1) while IVF does not overcome infertility but leaves this condition uncorrected, LTOT "restores" fertility — "that is, the ability to conceive and bear a child as a result of marital intercourse . . ."; and 2) while IVF transfers the initial step of generation from the interpersonal marriage act to a laboratory technique devoid of parental involvement, LTOT makes conception possible "in the interpersonal marriage act in a manner comparable to the surgical reconstruction of the Fallopian tube." Hence, he argues, "the genius of LTOT lies in its therapeutic function."

FATHER McCARTHY concludes that when Dr. McLaughlin's work "substantiates his expectations that LTOT is medically good therapy, it can be viewed as an exemplification of that part of Directive #21 of the *Ethical and Religious Directives for Catholic Health Facilities* which state that help 'may be given to a normally performed conjugal act to perform its purpose.'"

ONE FINAL point needs reaffirming here. It is that children who happen to be born through technological reproductive means — through "artificial fertilization," in the Instruction's idiom — are to be accorded no less respect and love than any other persons. In the unmistakably clear words of the Instruction: "Although the manner in which human conception is achieved with IVF and ET cannot be approved, every child who comes into the world must in any case be accepted as a living gift of the divine Goodness and must be brought up with love." (II, B, 5)

Needed Legislation

Part III of the final section of the Vatican's Instruction on the gift of life and the holiness of procreation largely constitutes an appeal both to society in general and nations in particular to uphold the inviolable right to life of every innocent human being, the rights of the family, the institution of marriage, and the dignity of human procreation.

THE INSTRUCTION specifically cites a need for laws to this effect. Recourse to informed consciences of individuals and to self-regulation by researchers cannot of itself ensure respect for personal rights and the public order. In fact, there is the possibility that the legislator's prerogatives in the whole area of bioethics might be usurped "by researchers claiming to govern humanity in the name of the biological discoveries and the alleged 'improvement' processes which they would draw from these discoveries. 'Eugenism' and forms of discrimination between human beings could come to be legitimized: this would constitute an act of violence and a serious offense to the equality, dignity and fundamental rights of the human person." (Instruction, III)

THE INTERVENTION of public authority in this regard must of course rest upon the rational principles that regulate the relationships between civil law and moral law. Civil law can never substitute for conscience, or dictate norms that transcend its competence. Further, "it must sometimes tolerate, for the sake of public order, things which it cannot prohibit without a greater evil's resulting." (Ibid.) However, the inalienable rights of each and every person must be recognized and respected by civil society and political authority; such rights pertain to human nature and inhere in the person by virtue of the creative act from which the person received his or her origin.

CRITICAL OF states that allow "the direct suppression of innocents" (e.g., abortion and its equivalent) and thus deny these innocents equality before the law, the Instruction likewise objects to political authority's approving the calling of human beings into existence through procedures that would expose them to the very grave risks cited above.

MOREOVER, the Instruction asks states to provide "appropriate penal sanctions for every deliberate violation of the child's rights." The law, it adds, must expressly forbid that human beings "even at the embryonic stage, should be treated as objects of experimentation, be mutilated or destroyed with the excuse that they are superfluous or incapable of developing normally." (Ibid.)

FURTHER STILL, civil law "cannot grant approval to techniques of artificial procreation which, for the benefit of third parties (doctors, biologists, economic or governmental powers), take away what is a right inherent in the relationship between spouses; and therefore, civil society cannot legalize the donation of gametes between persons who not legitimately united in marriage." (Ibid.)

TOO, legislation must prohibit, by virtue of the support that is due to the family, embryo banks, *post mortem* insemination, and "surrogate motherhood."

POLITICIANS are urged to commit themselves to secure respect for persons, for marriage, and for the family, to safeguard in society "the widest possible consensus on such essential points"; and to consolidate this consensus "whenever it risks being weakened or is in danger of collapse." (Ibid.)

IN THE face of the "undue legitimation" of unethical bioethical practices today, all men of good will are warned that they must commit themselves, especially within their own professional areas and in the exercise of their civil rights, to ensure "the reform of morally unacceptable civil laws and the correction of illicit practices." (Ibid.)

MOREOVER, conscientious objections vis-a-vis such laws must be supported and recognized: "a movement of passive resistance to the legitimation of practices contrary to human life and dignity is beginning to make an ever sharper impression among specialists in the biomedical sciences." (Ibid.)

THE CONCLUSION of the Instruction in six paragraphs, constitutes a plea to all those who, by reason of role and/or commitment, can help correct bioethical issues today. Not only writers, teachers, scientists, medical personnel, jurists and politicians, but also of course theologians, particularly ethicians, are urged to defend the holiness of sexuality, procreation and personhood — to defend man "against the excesses of his own power."

Extracorporeal Embryos

An example of new legislation to safeguard the gift of life was given by Father Donald McCarthy, testifying before a subcommittee of the House Science and Technology Committee in Washington, D.C., on 9 August 1984. Father McCarthy was then Director of the Pope John XXIII Medical-Moral Research and Education Center.

FATHER McCARTHY'S testimony related to the dignity and the rights of the human embryo. But he focused on a specifically nightmarish problem being debated on the international stage; namely, ethical questions linked to the creation and existence of extracorporeal embryos.

THAT the human embryo *is a human being* was readily granted, Father McCarthy reminded, by Dr. Robert Edwards, who helped bring into the world Louise Brown, the so-called "test-tube baby." The embryo, he said, is "a microscopic human being — one in its very earliest stages of development." Dr. Edwards' admission is in continuity with that of the lawyer convert of the third century. Tertullian, who in this context wrote: "The one who will be a man is already one."

SINCE 22 January 1973, Father McCarthy explained, the right to life of embryos in the United States is unprotected. Yet we of the United States, he went on, are committed in our democratic heritage to safeguard the rights of the weakest and most helpless members of society. Further, the class of human embryos under discussion before the Ethics Panel, i.e., those generated in a surrogate mother for flushing out and reimplantation within another mother, have — in Father McCarthy's words — "civil rights which need protection. In a free and democratic society we are called upon as responsible citizens to work for those rights rather than to acquiesce in technological violations of these rights."

SPECIFICALLY, Father McCarthy offered several suggestions in the area of legislative protection for extracorporeal embryos.

FIRST, legislation is indicated to prohibit any form of experimentation on a human embryo that is likely to injure or harm that embryo or to delay its natural development by retarding the time of its transfer and implantation; only procedures meant to benefit the embryo itself should be considered seriously for implementation.

SECONDLY, the freezing of human embryos — in any way — could be excluded by law. The reason here is not merely ignorance of long-term risks in such a procedure. Even without risk, "to subject the embryo to freezing without consent violates the dignity of the embryo unless freezing represented a proven kind of therapeutic procedure necessitated by the embryo's condition of health." Father McCarthy adds that we would not even think of freezing perfectly healthy babies after birth.

THIRDLY, any deliberate taking of the life of an extracorporeal embryo could be prohibited by law; likewise, any neglect of reasonable efforts to implant such an embryo in its mother's body.

FOURTHLY, removal of an inviable fetus or embryo from its mother's body for transfer to another woman could be prohibited by law as a form of experimental manipulation unless necessary to save the life of a fetus or embryo. (The assumption here is of course a *fait accompli.*)

THE FINAL suggestion made by Father McCarthy was that the law could readily prohibit "any parthenogenetic or uniparental procreation by cloning or any human-animal hybridization. No group of adults would seem to have the right to generate a human being by such procedures, which include among other objectionable features the deprival of natural parents for that human being (if indeed it were a human being)."

(ANOTHER suggestion had to do with IVF, though primarily from the legal aspect. "Many serious ethicists, myself included," Father McCarthy explained, "also believe that the very technique of *in vitro* fertilization violates the rights of human embryos on the ground that they have a right to be conceived in an act of personal self-giving and conjugal love rather than through a series of technical acts in a sterile laboratory.")

FATHER McCARTHY concluded by reminding the House subcommittee that childless marrieds deserve public support in the laudable efforts to become parents by means that do not violate the civil rights of embryos.

Part Two
The Medical Notes

by Leo T. Duffy, M.D.

Foreword

Relative to the subject matter covered in the following notes, I wish to stress that the medical material presented here, in the context of the recent Vatican Instruction on the gift of life and the holiness of procreation, is done so in the light of current medical opinions and practices; i.e., the medical state of the art. However, the procedures and opinions do not necessarily reflect my personal approval or endorsement. Coverage of all the moral and medical aspects should lay the groundwork for consideration and discussion of the topics set forth here. For the ethical or moral assessment, see the first part of this manual.

It is hoped that the offering of the following background material will provide readers with an up-to-date knowledge in this subject, and will also enable counsellors to confidently approach a medical-ethical dialogue on these subjects.

Through the foresight of the Philosophy and Theology Departments at Holy Apostles College and Seminary in Cromwell, Connecticut, this coverage has been provided over the past several years. The subject matter which follows is a revised and limited compilation of the lectures given to graduate students in the interdisciplinary bioethics course at Holy Apostles College and Seminary, and is adapted to enhance the moral and medical aspects of bioethics.

A glossary, with derivations, is also included to ensure understanding the medical terminology used.

Leo T. Duffy, M.D.
July 1987

Chapter I
Procreation

(For the ethical dimensions of the following, consult Part I of this Manual)

FERTILIZATION —

The propagation of the human race, as we will consider it under the circumstances of a marital relationship, depends on the procreative (life-giving) abilities of the partners. Basically, fertilization (or conception) occurs at the moment that the wall of the female ovum (egg) is penetrated by the male spermatozoon (sperm cell).

In the male, the process for the production of the sperm cells begins in the testicles under the stimulating effect of certain hormones. The sperm cells are passed through an organ, overlying the testicle, called the epididymis. The cells, plus an accumulation of other fluid from adjacent glands, become the seminal fluid which passes through the vas deferens into the seminal vesicles. At the time of intercourse, the seminal vesicles are stimulated to eject their contents into the male urethral canal, and finally end up as a sperm-bearing ejaculate deposited into the female vagina.

In the female, the uterus, Fallopian tubes, and ovaries are located in the lower abdominal cavity (pelvic cavity). The uterus is approximately the size of a large pear. It consists of a fundus (top), a corpus (body), and a cervix, this latter being the portion which extends into the vagina. The canal which passes through the cervix extends from the opening in the vaginal end (the cervical os) into the uterine cavity. The lining of the uterus is called the endometrium. This tissue is desquamated (shed) at menstruation and regenerates during the monthly intervals. It is the site for the implantation of a fertilized ovum. The tubes are the tubular canals which connect the fundus of the uterus to the pelvic cavity and provide the means for the sperm and ovum to unite. The pelvic fimbriated ends of the tubes collect the ovum when it is released from the ovary (ovulation), at about the 14th day of the menstrual cycle. Each of the two ovaries is about the size of an English walnut and each is located as an attachment to the uterus just below each tube.

The normal course of fertilization takes place when, through the coital act, the male ejaculates seminal fluid into the vaginal canal of the female partner. The sperm cells then ascend through the uterine cervical canal, through the uterine cavity, and enter the Fallopian tubes. The female ovum, when released from the ovary, enters the pelvic end of the tube to meet and fertilize with a sperm cell. From about Day 1 to Day 3 the fertilized egg (zygote) develops to a 16 cell stage (morula). This developing organism then moves along the tube to enter the uterine cavity. During Day 5 to Day 6, it remains as a free blastocyst. It then begins the process of embedding itself into the uterine lining (endometrium) from about Day 6 to Day 7. By Day 7 the organism is usually well embedded, and now has begun the formation of the placenta which becomes the source of vascular nourishment. The embryo enlarges and develops over an average period of 266 days to reach full term (280 days from the last menstrual period). There are occasions when the implantation of the fertilized ovum may occur at an abnormal site (ectopic pregnancy), such as on the tubal lining (tubal pregnancy), or the abdominal-pelvic structures (abdominal pregnancy).

INFERTILITY —

Unfortunately, there are occasions where one or the other, or both, partners are inflicted with impediments to the process of fertilization. In 1965 about 73% of couples in the childbearing ages were able to have children. Because of selective sterilization this total has declined to 52.7% by 1982. A health statistic report[1] in 1985 reveals that, of 54 million women of childbearing age (15-44 yrs.) in 1982, 4.4 million had an impairment other than sterilization that made it difficult or impossible to have children. In all, about 13 million women had impaired or total inability to have children for reasons other than intended sterility. These hindrances may be temporary or permanent in nature.

In the male, there may exist various physical or psychological conditions which result in an inability to engage in normal, ejaculatory, coital relationships; or there may be an interference in the production, qualities, or quantities of sperm cells. A defect in the male is estimated to be the infertility factor in 20-40% of the cases. Examples are:

1) *varicocele* — this consists of varying degrees of varicosities, usually on the left, involving the spermatic cord, or testicular area, which may also interfere with the normal production of sperm cells.

2) *hydrocele* — this is an abnormal collection of a watery fluid in the testicular area which may also affect sperm production.

3) *hypospadias* — an abnormal location of the penile opening (meatus) on the underside of the penis. This may prevent the deposition of the seminal fluid into a favorable location within the vaginal canal. Location of the meatus on the upper surface of the penis is called an *epispadias*.

4) *premature ejaculation* — for various reasons, such as chronic drug usage, fatigue, or the impact of psychogenic factors, the male may be subject to a seminal ejacu-

lation before vaginal penetration has been accomplished.

5) *retrograde ejaculation* — an unusual anomaly due to the distortion of the urethral canal which may misdirect the semen back into the bladder.

6) *endocrine gland deficiencies* — these are rare, but may be due to glandular malfunction, such as the thyroid.

7) *impotence* — a persistent inability to sustain a penile erection in order to accomplish a normal, coital relationship. It may result from chronic drug or alcohol usage, or often is due to psychological factors.

8) *low virility* — this may be present in various forms relating to the degree, and caliber, of sperm cell production. It may amount to a total lack of sperm cells in the seminal fluid (azoospermia); or there may be a reduction in the normal number of sperm (oligospermia). The normal number of cells average 60-120 million per cubic centimeter (about ¼ teaspoon) of seminal fluid, although pregnancy has occurred with counts of only 20 million. A total seminal ejaculate may exceed 500 million sperm cells. The sperm present may show diminished or poor motility (60%); and deformed shapes of the cells (60%) may also be present. The seminal fluid, which transports the sperm cells, may also be deficient in amount or volume. This impaired virility may be the result of certain past or underlying diseases, chemical intoxication, or advancing age.

The anatomical anomalies noted are often amenable to corrective surgery. Two of the causes, impotence and low virility, are the most common; but are also amenable to appropriate therapeutic efforts.

In the female, there also exist various physical and/or psychological conditions which preclude the union of the male sperm with the female ovum. Examples are:

1) *imperforate hymen* — the tissue which usually

partially occludes the opening to the vaginal canal may be totally intact.

2) *congenital anomalies* — there may be an absence, or maldevelopment, of the female genitalia, e.g., the cervix, uterus, or tubes.

3) *cervical stenosis* — the canal from the vagina connecting to the uterine cavity may be partially closed.

4) *tubal occlusion* — there may be a blockage of the tubal canals. This is most often due to inflammation, and is called pelvic inflammatory disease (PID). It prevents passage of the sperm into the tube, or the passage of the ovum to unite with the sperm cell. The inflammation is most often due as the results of venereal diseases, such as chlamydia (50%), or gonorrhea (25%). Adhesions from a condition called endometriosis may also cause scarring or distortion of the tubal structures.

5) *uterine fibroids* — these are benign tumors located outside the cavity, in the wall, or on the outer surface of the uterus, causing distortion.

6) *glandular dysfunction* — hormonal imbalances due to ovarian, pituitary, adrenal, or thyroid dysfunction.

7) *constitutional disease* — such as diabetes.

8) *psychological disorders* — such as frigidity, and abnormal pain with vaginal spasm during intercourse (vaginismus).

9) *elective delay* — because of the pressure of maintaining a career status, a woman may elect to delay having children until an age when ovarian function may be on the wane.

10) *cervical mucus* — the mucus normally present at the cervical opening may have an antagonistic effect on the sperm cells.

11) *strenuous athletics* — prolonged running, jogging, dancing, etc. may affect the hormonal balance. For example, a marked loss of fatty tissue may affect the storage of estrogen.

12) *mental stress* — may affect and suppress ovulation.
13) *exposure to certain occupational hazard.*
14) *hyperprolactinemia* (hPRL) — a marked increase in this hormonal product of the anterior pituitary gland has been found to have a hindering effect on the physiology of the ovary.

If pregnancy fails to occur through the usual coital act, which is performed at the optimal time of ovulation, a proper and thorough medical evaluation must be made to determine the status, or even existence, of infertility. If it is determined that obstacles exist, then appropriate corrective measures should be instituted. Of about 95% of the couples that are diagnosed as infertile, there are about 50% who offer a good prognosis for successful therapy. When there is no response to such measures, certain artificial alternatives to natural coitus have been proposed for consideration:

I. *Artificial Insemination*
   a) husband's sperm to his spouse (AIH)
   b) husband's sperm to a surrogate ovum vector who will carry the child to term and delivery (surrogate mother).
   c) husband's sperm to a surrogate vector from whom the embryo will be removed, and transferred to the spouse (embryo transfer).
II. *Artificial Insemination by Sperm Vector* (AIV)
III. *"In Vitro" Fertilization* (IVF)
IV. *Tubal Ovum Transfer* (TOT)
V. *Gamete Intrafallopian Transfer* (GIFT)
VI. *Cloning*

Again, the following analyses do not reflect ethical values per se; for ethical assessments, consult the first portion of the Manual.

I. *Artificial Insemination*

a) *Husband's sperm to spouse (AIH)* — the medical "need" and application of this method became apparent when, for various physical and/or psychological conditions affecting the male partner, an inability to fulfill normal ejaculatory relationship was encountered. There are certain methods recommended by physicians in order to obtain the seminal specimen which is to be used for the insemination. (There are of course moral objections raised concerning some of the methods used for this purpose.) The methods are:

1) *masturbation*

2) *condom* — some physicians suggest placing a pinhole in the condom to overcome the moral objection to the use of a contraceptive.

3) *coitus interruptus* — this is an interruption in the coital act when ejaculation is imminent. After withdrawal of the penis, the ejaculate is deposited into a small jar.

4) *prostatic massage* — this requires a rectal approach whereby the doctor inserts a finger in the rectum, and by palpation and massage of the prostate gland, the seminal vesicles are stimulated to discharge their stored seminal fluid through the urethral canal. The specimen is caught in a jar.

The techniques for insemination essentially follow a set routine. The seminal specimen, which is brought to the doctor's office shortly after it is obtained, is drawn up into a syringe-like plastic tube. The contents are sprayed directly at the opening of the cervical canal (os) of the female recipient. From this point the sperm should migrate up the canal into the uterine cavity. Sometimes additional seminal fluid is placed into a cervical cap (or Spoon) which is retained over the os for several hours before removal. The insemination technique usually is performed twice in the same month, just before and just after ovulation. There are several means to determine the occurrence of ovulation.

b) *Husband's sperm to surrogate ovum vector* (mother) — the impregnation of the woman who is to bear the child, is accomplished by using the sperm of the male partner of the couple desiring the child. This is an example of artificial insemination *to (or of)* a vector. In this relationship, the vector of the ovum is not the spouse of the male sperm donor. In the management of such a pregnancy, and in any clinical intervention that might be needed, the surrogate mother should be the source of consent. Complex problems arise from this procedure, as have become evident in the well-publicized "Whitehead Case," and the legal entanglements that have ensued. It is difficult to separate payment for the services of carrying and bearing a child, from the payment *for* a child — the latter being illegal. Questions about illegitimacy have not been resolved. Payment, other than expenses to the surrogate mother, can create a potential for exploitation. Similar to the selection of male vectors, a surrogate mother should be screened physically, and include a medical history and genetic background. It is estimated that over 150 surrogate mother infants have been born in the United States. There is no statistical knowledge to date relating to the psychological stress which might involve all parties concerned.

c) *Husband's sperm to surrogate ovum vector (for embryo transfer - ET)* — this method involves the procedure which has also been called "surrogate embryo transfer" (SET). The surrogate female is selected for artificial insemination by the sperm of the husband of the spouse. This spouse will be the eventual recipient of the embryo. Following the insemination, four or five days are allowed to elapse for fertilization to take place; and to allow the fertilized egg to move into the uterine cavity. The uterine cavity is then flushed out with a special fluid in order to obtain the very early free embryo. This would represent an embryo formation of about 100 cells, if the procedure was successful up to this point. The embryo is inspected under magnification for any possible abnormalities. If normal in appearance, it is transferred into the uterine cavity of the recipient spouse using the same technique as in IVF. The spouse is usually one who cannot become pregnant because of the lack of ovaries, or of ovarian function. Therefore, before transferring the embryo to the spouse, she will require priming with ovarian hormones. This method has been successful many times with rhesus monkeys, and there have also been several successes in humans. The cost for the procedure is about $5,000 (1987). The complications could be a tubal pregnancy, and of more significance, an accidental pregnancy in the ovum donor due to non-recovery of the embryo. Concerning the use of frozen embryos — about 30-50% fail to survive. However those that do have a better chance of successful pregnancy probably because the recipient has not had recent artificial hormonal stimulation, which can unfavorably alter the female endometrial lining.

There has also been a successful use of a combination of the IVF procedure, and a surrogate mother, whereby the husband's sperm is incubated with ova taken from the spouse. The resultant embryo is transferred to the uterus of the female who is to act as the surrogate mother. The developing embryo is carried to full-term and delivered from the surrogate. This has been used in cases where the spouse has had a hysterectomy, but functioning ovaries have been preserved. The surrogate mother has not contributed any chromosomes to this embryo, and has been used primarily as a storehouse for the developing embryo while she provides the necessary nutrients and environment for the proper development of the growing fetus.

II. *Artificial Insemination by Sperm Vector (AIV)* — the use of this method of artificial insemination involves the participation of a *male third party*, and is selected in the situations where the husband is unable to fertilize his spouse, usually due to a defective sperm supply. The seminal specimen received from a third party vector should be of recent origin, although frozen specimens from sperm banks have been used with success. The insemination follows the same technique as in AIH. It is of prime importance to make a careful surveillance of potential vectors to rule out current physical disease, hereditary diseases, recurrent disease, hepatitis, venereal disease, AIDS, etc. An attempt should be made to appropriately match in the areas of hair and eye color, body build, race and blood type. The submitted specimen must also be examined to ensure good sperm quality. The uses of AIV are mainly limited to instances where the husband is totally infertile, or has had a vasectomy. It is also considered where the possibility of inherited disease exists, such as cystic fibrosis, hemophilia, Tay-Sachs (Jewish race), sickle-cell anemia (black race), or thalassemia (Mediterranean race).

Each year it is estimated that 6,000-10,000 couples elect to try AIV. One study showed that it took an average of about six menstrual cycles to produce conception. About 91% conceived within the first year, and 74% within the first six months. The overall pregnancy rate was 72%. Those having difficulty in conceiving were more likely to require medication to stimulate ovulation.

A serious issue to be considered is the maintenance of vector and recipient anonymity. The American Fertility Society has provided guidelines for the use of AIV. These are designed to avert legal complications apparent at this time, or foreseen in the future.

III. *"In Vitro" Fertilization* (IVF) — Patrick Steptoe,

M.D., and Robert Edwards, Ph.D., British scientists, were the pioneers in the research involving fertilization of a human ovum under laboratory conditions outside of the human uterus. Their initial success occurred in 1978 with the eventual production of a live baby (Louise Brown), by the use of IVF. Up to 1986 over 1000 live babies have been delivered. Twins, triplets, and quadruplets have been produced. At present there are over 200 IVF clinics in the world.

Obviously, the initial step in IVF requires the procurement of a normal, mature ovum. Stimulation of the ovary to produce such ova (ovulation), may be accomplished by the cyclic administration of certain hormones. An example of such a technique is to give the patient a hormone, such as "CLOMID" or "PERGONAL" to promote follicle development in the ovary. Such development may be monitored by the use of ultrasound, or by measurement of the luteinizing hormone which is obtained from a specimen of the patient's urine. About the 14th to 16th day of the menstrual cycle, another hormone, human chorionic gonadtrophin (HCG) which is derived from placental tissue, is injected to "ripen" the ovum, or ova. Then, under local or light general anesthesia, a small incision is made in the abdominal wall of the patient just below the umbilicus. Through this incision a small instrument, which provides magnification and illumination, is inserted, and the ovaries are visualized. Maturing follicles, located on the surface of the ovaries, are identified. The visualization of the ovaries may also be accomplished by the insertion of a needle under ultrasonic guidance after local anesthesia of the abdominal wall. The needle is guided to the ripe ovarian follicles by following the path described on the viewing screen. With this technique, the patient is free to leave within an hour with no discomfort or residual disability. By means of a Teflon-coated needle, the follicles are aspirated to obtain the ovum contained within.

After washing, the ovum is placed in a culture plate which contains a special growth medium. Following about four to eight hours of incubation, a specimen of sperm is added to the culture. At various intervals, the incubated specimen is examined microscopically to determine the rate of pronuclei development, i.e., the rate of cell division. When the cleavage reaches an 8-cell stage, usually 38-50 hours, the embryo is transferred to the unanesthetized patient by means of a catheter which is inserted through the cervical canal into the uterine cavity. The embryo is injected from the catheter to lie freely within the uterine cavity with the expectation that it will attach itself to the uterine wall (endometrium), to further grow and develop. The follow-up to ascertain successful implantation is similar to that used to document pregnancy in normal circumstances, e.g., positive pregnancy tests, amenorrhea, uterine enlargement, etc.

A simplified version of IVF has been introduced as a claimed means of eliminating ethical and moral dilemmas presented by the transfer of a single ovum to the uterus, disregarding others that may be present. The newer method transfers all of the eggs and sperm which are in the culture medium, rather than selective transfer of a single ovum. At Yale School of Medicine this method results in a pregnancy about once in every five attempts, or 20%. The chances increase to 28% with two embryos, and 38% with three embryos. The procedure costs between $3000-5000. Only about 25% of the males in these infertile couples have sperm counts high enough to qualify. The criteria at the University of Connecticut Health Center for IVF program acceptance are: 1) irreparable tubal damage, 2) oligospermia of 10 million or above, 3) unexplained infertility of greater than three years, and 4) a female less than 41 years of age. No surrogate vendors are used even if the husband is infertile.

The American Infertility Society has recommended the recognition of IVF as an acceptable treatment for women with absent or damaged Fallopian tubes. (For the ethical assessment, see Part I of this Manual.) Success rate, now about 60% with carefully chosen candidates, is said to help a great many infertile couples achieve a successful pregnancy, and will limit the number of children with congenital anomalies because of inherited genetic defects. Again, however, for the ethical assessment, consult the theological analyses of the Vatican Instruction on "The Gift of Life," in the first portion of this Manual.

With respect to complications, there is no evidence to date that this procedure increases fetal anomalies. A rare complication might be a tubal pregnancy. Finally, there has been some concern regarding an adverse psychological impact on the involved couples, and/or the vectors and physicians. This may be related to the secrecy surrounding the procedure, and the lack of legal guidelines. It is becoming increasingly obvious that additional psychological research is required to cope with the emerging problems confronting surrogate mothers, the parental couples, and especially the children resulting from such conceptions. No one knows the impact on a child who eventually learns that several thousand dollars have been paid by his "parents" in order that he/she might become a member of the family through such an unorthodox procedure.

IV. *Tubal Ovum Transfer* (TOT) — this method of fertilization was developed at the National Institutes of Health (NIH) using monkeys as test animals. The initial success rate was 16%, as compared to a rate of 15-20% in human couples of normal fertility in a single menstrual cycle. The use of this method is especially applicable to women who have had tubal disease or surgery. TOT involves the removal of a mature ovum from the spouse by laparoscopy, as is done in IVF. The ovum is then deposited by injection into any portion of the tube remaining attached to the uterus, or directly into the uterus through the uterine wall. After a few days, impregnation is attempted by the husband by means of the coital act. This procedure thereby allows both fertilization and incubation to occur in the uterus (that is "in-vivo") thus alleviating moral and ethical concerns which are raised with the use of IVF. Several Catholic, and other Church authorities and theologians, have concurred that the procedure of TOT is in accord with the teachings of the Catholic Church; for a specific ethical assessment, see the first part of this Manual.

V. *Gamete Intrafallopian Tube Transfer* (GIFT) — this procedure involves the placement, via laparoscopy, of both the sperm and the egg into the Fallopian tube when at least one tube is patent. After hormonal treatment of the spouse in order to induce follicular development, the egg specimens are obtained by aspiration from the follicles. The sperm specimen, having been obtained about 2½ hours previously, has been prepared to yield a sperm concentration of 100,000/25 milliliters. The implantation catheter is loaded successively with 25 cc. of the sperm preparation, an air space of 5 cc., 2 eggs loaded in a volume of 25 cc., another air space of 5 cc., and finally 1 cc. of the medium. This preparation is placed, by laparoscopy, into the open fimbriated end of the Fallopian tube, and injected. One report shows a pregnancy rate of 27%, with none reported as going to term.

The claimed advantages are:

1) acceptance by some major religions
2) avoidance of extracorporeal incubation
3) physiologic entry of the embryo into the uterine cavity

The disadvantages are:
1) inability to determine if fertilization has taken place in the absence of an established pregnancy.
2) a theoretical risk of increased ectopic pregnancy, and tubal infection.
3) possible increase in multiple gestation.

For the ethical assessment, see the first part of this Manual.

A variation of adoption has emerged through the use of "embryo adoption." This is accomplished by the in-vitro fertilization of an ovum supplied by the female vector, and united with the sperm supplied by the male vector. The resulting embryo is implanted in the uterus of the recipient desiring the child; or the vector sperm may be used by insemination into the uterus of the female vector who supplies the ovum. The resulting fertilized ovum is flushed from the female vector's uterus, as is done in surrogate embryo transfer (ET). The embryo is then implanted into the uterus of the mother-to-be.

VII. *Cloning* — this is mentioned only to complete these outlines of some methods of fertilization. It is more appropriate in the field of veterinary medicine than in any application to humans. However, a definition should suffice to indicate what such a procedure contemplates and indicates. *Cloning represents an exact, genetic duplication of a single individual.* It involves the transfer of chromosomes from a body cell of an individual to an ovum from which the existing chromatin material has been previously removed. This ovum, under optimal conditions, is expected to develop to produce an individual with the same genetic characteristics, and physical appearance, as the donor of the body cell.

The above outline of the Alternative Selections for procreation represents several current practices. However, there are certain to be investigations into other modes of accomplishing the union of the male sperm and the female ovum, in a proper environment, to attain the goal of a fully developed, healthy offspring. Of necessity, these practices undoubtedly raise questions concerning the moral, ethical, and legal implications of the procedures, questions which are clearly addressed in the Vatican Instruction on "The Gift of Life."

Table One[7]

STATISTICS RELATIVE TO IN VITRO FERTILIZATION (152 patients)

Retrieval of an ovum	85% (130)
Fertilization occurred	79% (103)
	68% (152)
Embryo sufficiently developed	88% (91)
	60% (152)
Pregnancies occurred	16% (15)
	10% (152)

STATISTICS RELATIVE TO HUMAN REPRODUCTION

Chance of fertilization after exposure to sperm	85%
Lost within two weeks (occult pregnancies)	50%
Subsequently lost	25%
Theoretical probability of live birth	30%
Probability after single exposure	25%

Table Two[8]

BASIC OUTLINE FOR TECHNOLOGICAL REPRODUCTION
(for detailed explanation, refer to the pertinent sections of Chapter Two, and the Glossary)

I. *Use by Husband and Spouse* (homologous artificial insemination) (AIH).

a) *In-Vivo Fertilization* — this is accomplished by catheter instillation of a specimen of the husband's semen into the uterus of the spouse by the vaginal route.

b) *"In Vitro" Fertilization* (IVF) — an ovum (or ova) obtained from the spouse by laparoscopy is placed in a glass laboratory dish which contains nutrient media. Later, a specimen of the husband's semen is added to the dish. After the union of the sperm and ovum, cell division occurs to form an embryo. At a certain stage of development, the embryo is transferred to the spouse by means of a catheter inserted through the vagina into the uterus where the embryo is deposited.

c) *Tubal Ovum Transfer* (TOT) — this requires removal of an ovum, by laparoscopy, from the ovary of the spouse. The ovum is then injected into the Fallopian tube (or uterus) of the spouse. After a few days, impregnation is attempted by the husband through the coital act.

d) *Gamete Intrafallopian Tube Transfer* (GIFT) — the husband's semen is combined in a catheter with the ovum obtained by laparoscopy from the spouse. Nutrient media is added. These contents are injected into the Fallopian tube of the spouse. If fertilization of the ovum occurs, it should migrate to the uterine cavity to embed in the endometrial wall.

II. *Use by Surrogate*

a) *Artificial Insemination* (AI) — this is accomplished as in "*In Vivo*" Fertilization, except that the insemination is done to a surrogate female who is to eventually bear the child, and who is the vendor (supplier) of the ovum. This is a *heterologous* transfer.

b) *Surrogate Embryo Transfer* (SET) — by this method the surrogate who supplies the ovum is inseminated with the husband's semen. After several days, while the developing embryo is still unattached, the uterus is flushed out to obtain the embryo (if pregnancy occurred). The embryo is then transferred by catheter to the uterus of the spouse. Genetically, the husband and the surrogate have supplied the chromosomes as in A1 above. This is a *heterologous* transfer.

c) *Embryo transfer* (ET from spouse) — by this method, an embryo is developed by IVF using the husband's semen, and ova from the spouse. The embryo is transferred from the dish to the surrogate mother who is to carry the fetus to full-term. Genetically, the husband and the spouse have supplied the chromosomes through their gametes (sperm and ova). The surrogate has been the supplier of a "nutrient incubator," and has no input into the genetic phenotype of the fetus. This is a *homologous* transfer.

III. *Use by Vendor* (heterologous transfer) — this method supplies semen, fresh or frozen, by a third party. It can be used in any of the above methods where sperm are required for impregnation. It is noted that in some cases the surrogate becomes a vendor in the sense that she supplies the ovum.

References

1. National Center for Health Statistics (1982)
2. IVF Program, Univ. Conn. Health Center
3. IVF and Alternatives (LTOT); Gary Hodgen, PhD., JAMA, Aug. 7, 1981; Vol. 246, No. 6.
4. Tufts Med. Alumni Bull., Fall 1985; A. Ruciano, M.D.
5. J. Reproductive Med., Vol. 3, No. 4, 1986; S. L. Corson, M.D., et al.
6. Int. J. Fertility, 30:41-45, 1985; R. H. Asch, et al.
7. TABLE ONE — IVF Statistics.
8. TABLE TWO — Basic Outline for Technological Reproduction.

Chapter II
Abortion

(The ethical aspects of direct abortion, which is of course intrinsically evil, are discussed in the first portion of this Manual.)

The term abortion, or miscarriage, for the purposes of the Manual, pertains to giving birth to an embryo or fetus prior to the stage of viability, i.e., before 20 weeks of gestation, or with a weight of less than 400-500 grams. After 20 weeks of gestation, or above 400-500 grams weight, the term "premature birth" is used. Abortions may also be classified as follows:

a) complete — where the entire uterine contents have been passed, i.e., the embryo, membranes and placenta.

b) habitual — where there have been three or more spontaneous consecutive embryonic or fetal losses.

c) incomplete — where only portions of the conceptus have been passed.

d) induced — where evacuation of the uterine cavity is brought about by the use of drugs and/or mechanical means. The term "therapeutic" is also used when the induction is performed for the sake of the mother's health. This is the classification which most often raises moral/ethical/legal questions.

e) inevitable — where the membranes rupture, and the cervix is dilating, and becomes incompetent to retain the fetus in-utero.

f) missed — where the fetus dies "in utero," and is retained for two months or longer. In this situation, the rare development of a lithopedion (stone/child) may occur.

g) spontaneous (natural) — where no medical or

surgical means have been used.

h) threatened — where crampy uterine pains, and vaginal bleeding occur, but no pregnancy tissue is passed.

The "indications" for induced abortions, in the present state of society, are often cited as the following:
a) economic
b) immaturity (age)
c) social
d) health
e) genetic
f) rape or incest

It is in the genetic area that a great deal of stress has been placed. In a study of chromosomal abnormalities, e.g., Down's syndrome, an amniocentesis at 16-20 weeks, at the maternal age of 35+ years, showed eight fetuses had chromosomal defects. Alpha-feto-protein (AFP) levels (elevation of which suggests a fetal anomaly) were normal, and no neural defects were apparent. Out of the eight at birth, four had Down's syndrome, one had an anomaly associated with mental retardation. Three, with less severe chromosomal anomalies, were apparently normal at birth. Further discussion of this subject will be covered under genetic therapy, and amniocentesis.

The mechanics usually undertaken for the accomplishment of an abortion are medical and/or surgical.

SUMMARY:
THE FIRST TWELVE WEEKS

As 91 percent of abortions within the United States, for example, occur within the first 12 weeks of pregnancy, let's look at fetal development of the unborn.
- **18 days** The beating heart already pumps blood through its own bloodstream.

- **Five weeks** The nose and cheeks appear and fingers are faintly visible.
- **Six weeks** The nervous system begins to function. Beginnings of the skeleton, the kidneys, stomach and liver begin working.
- **Seven weeks** The unborn child has its own brain waves. (Brain waves are among the legal criteria that determine whether a person is alive or not.) The tiny baby has all its outer and inner organs. It has a face with eyes, nose, lips and tongue.
- **Nine and 10 weeks** The thyroid and adrenal glands function. The baby can squint, swallow, and respond to noise.
- **10 weeks** The unborn basically has everything found in newborns.
- **12 weeks** The completely formed fingerprints will not change except for size. The little boy or girl now is more than 3 inches long and weighs about an ounce. For this tiny baby all that remains is growth.

Under medical techniques the following means are used:

a) *Prostaglandins* (20 carbon compounds) — two of these products are known as PGF2a, and PGE2. The first compound is used in an injectable form, and is administered by instillation into the amniotic cavity. The second compound is used as a vaginal suppository. The effect of these products is to promote uterine contractions, and thereby terminate the pregnancy. The technique is usually instituted between 13 to 24 weeks pregnancy which is a time when surgical means are hazardous. The complications are:

1) severe labor pains
2) pharmacological side-effects (hypersensitivity)
3) contraindications because of preexisting conditions

such as cardio-vascular disease, hypertension, and gastric ulcers.

4) failure rate of between 2-8%.

5) delivery of a living fetus. One author has suggested avoiding this possibility by intra-amniotic injection of urea (thereby killing the fetus) before the use of these compounds.

b) *Hypertonic Saline* — this is injected intra-amniotically. The method may be complicated by intraperitoneal or uterine necrosis (tissue breakdown), or may result in shock from the sodium overload.

c) *Hypertonic Urea* — this intra-amniotic injection may be complicated by nausea, vomiting, myonecrosis (muscle death) of the uterine wall, tachycardia, shock, or coagulation defect from a release of thromboplastin. The infusion methods have a complication rate varying from 7 to 25%.

d) *Hormones* (morning-after pill) — e.g., after rape.

Under surgical techniques the following are used:

a) *Prostaglandins* may be administered a few hours before surgery as a means of softening the cervix so the cervical canal may be dilated more easily. Also laminaria tents, which are composed of dried seaweed made in the shape of a cylindrical tube, may be inserted in the cervical canal where they swell and cause a gradual dilation of the canal.

b) *Dilation and Evacuation* (D&E) — this involves dilating the cervical canal to facilitate the insertion of a sharp curet or crushing forceps into the uterine cavity to remove the fetus. A suction cannula is also used for this purpose. Complications from such a procedure may be bleeding, uterine perforation, cervical lacerations (3.4%), infection (3.9%), and the possibility of future spontaneous abortions or sterility[1].

c) *Vaginal or abdominal surgery* to evacuate the uterine contents by incision into the uterus (hysterotomy). The complications are those that may occur with any traumatic uterine surgery associated with a pregnancy, namely infection, bleeding and lacerations. The matter of an adverse psychological impact is also a serious consideration which must be dealt with in many post-abortion situations.

The complications of abortions have further been reported as shown in the following statistics:
1) the rates of major complications in teenagers from induced abortion were generally lower than for older women; although there was an increased risk of cervical injury during suction-curettage procedures. Center for Disease Control data showed that the rates of major complications in teenagers were one to three per 1000 suction-curettage procedures, and approximately 13 per 1000 saline-administration procedures. The death-to-case rate for teenagers was 1.3 per 100,000 abortions[2].
2) women with Chlamydia trachomatis infection in the cervix at the time of therapeutic abortion are at the risk of developing postoperative pelvic inflammatory disease (PID), as shown by an occurrence rate of 20%. Therefore a culture, and if necessary, a treatment of this condition, is recommended before any abortive procedure[3].
3) women who have had either a spontaneous abortion, or an induced abortion, are more likely to have a second trimester spontaneous abortion in a subsequent pregnancy[4].
4) complications in infusion abortion range from 7-25%. Besides fever, cramping, heavy bleeding and large clots, complications include fertility problems due to uterine infection or injury, and an increase in the rate of miscarriage due to cervical incompetence. The mortality rates for 8-week abortions is 0.5/100,000 procedures.

This rate increases to 7/100,000 at 13-15 weeks, and to 20/100,000 at 16 weeks and beyond. This compared to 14.5/100,000 for term childbirth. In 1980, 10% of abortions were done in the second trimester, and they accounted for half of the deaths reported[5].

5) the use of laminaria and subsequent urea amnioinfusion in second trimester patients resulted in blood loss of over 500 cc. in 2.1%; over 1000 cc. in 5%; intravascular clots in 1%; uterine perforation in 1%; infection in 6%; incomplete procedures in 18%; retained products requiring repeat surgery in 7%; and blood transfusions in 30%[6].

6) relative to the above study, a commentary was made by a reviewer to the effect that viability now hovers between 24 to 26 weeks from the last menstrual period, and some fetuses have been reported to survive without serious sequelae. He believes physicians should take into account the legal requirements, and moral and ethical aspects, instead of what is technically feasible and the fundamental criterion in decisions about abortion. From the psychological point of view, experience has shown that patients who do not seek to interrupt their pregnancy until late in the second trimester, are quite ambivalent about the decision. One report stated that up to one percent of patients who had to wait an average of 10 days after the request for a second trimester abortion, changed their minds, and carried to term. The possible long-term psychological impact on these patients, because of interruption at such a late stage of pregnancy, should not be underestimated[7].

References

1. OBGYN Literature News; Vol. 3, No. 6, 1983
2. "The Risks Associated with Teenage Abortion"; Cates, W.J. et al; N. Eng. Jour. Med.; 309:621-624, 1983.
3. "PID Associated with Chlamydia trachomatis Infection after Therapeutic Abortion"; Brit. Jour. of Venereal Diseases; 59:189-192, 1983.
4. "The Relationship between Spontaneous and Induced Abortions in Subsequent Pregnancies"; European Jour. of Obs-Gyn, and Reproductive Biology; 14:299-309, 1983.
5. D. S. Glucken, M.D., et al; Mademoiselle; 89/10:166, October 1983.
6. "Serial Multiple Laminaria and Adjunctive Urea in Abortion", OB-GYN, 63:543-548, 1984.
7. "Commentary", Dr. Gorten; Intelligence Reports in OBS-GYN; Sept. 1984.

Chapter III
Genetics

(For moral aspects, see first part of this Manual.)

Genetics is a branch of science that deals with *natural development*, as distinct from *Eugenics* which is the science of development through *artificial selection*. The latter is classified as positive or negative, e.g.:

1) *positive eugenics* embodies efforts to improve a genetic heritage. Artificial (donor) insemination has been used as a method to accomplish this end, especially as applied to animals. Other techniques considered are IVF, sperm/ovum banks, and genetic engineering.

2) *negative eugenics* is utilized for the prevention of the transmissions of genetically-induced disorders to a future generation. Methods to accomplish this purpose include genetic engineering, sterilization, contraception, abortion, and planned parenthood. (Again, for the moral aspects, see the first part of this Manual.)

Historically[1], the basic work for modern genetics began in 1866 through the studies of Gregor Mendel, an Austrian monk. He found that variations in plants (peas) were controlled by a single physical *factor*, which is now known as a *gene*. He also determined that certain traits were *dominant*, or *recessive*. Later, in the 1920's, it was learned that genes are positioned upon thread-like structures called *chromosomes* which are located in the nucleus of each cell. In 1944[2], the basic material for hereditary changes was identified as deoxyribonucleic acid (DNA). In 1953[3], the double-helix structure of DNA was discovered. In 1970[4], scientists discovered a method of slicing molecules by the use of a "restrictive enzyme"; and in 1972[5], they combined the DNA from two viruses

— thus forming the so-called "recombinant DNA". In 1973[6], recombinant DNA was inserted into bacteria that reproduce (or clone) the foreign DNA. Thus the age of genetic engineering began for the reason that bacteria modified with foreign genes operate like very efficient photocopying machines, churning out limitless copies of the gene. One scientist[7] compared gene-cloning to cutting a printed paper in half, inserting a new paragraph in the middle, then photocopying the altered version over and over to reproduce the new material. In 1979, bacteria were programmed to turn out human growth hormones, which previously had been scarce, and costly to produce. Insulin and interferon came next.

A brief review of the chromosomal fundamentals of genetics might be in order at this point, without going into any depth. In human genetics, the basis lies in the existence of a *male gamete* (or sperm cell), and the *female gamete* (or ovum). The union of these two, under the proper circumstances, produces a *zygote* (or fertilized egg). The zygote continues by cell division (mitosis), to form the *embryo*, and eventually a *fetus*. Each gamete contains in its nucleus, small bodies called *chromosomes*. These chromosomes are composed of *genes* with deoxyribonucleic acid strands. Herein lie the sources, or carriers, of hereditary traits. Each gamete contains 22 somatic (body) chromosomes, plus one sex chromosome for a total of 23 chromosomes — a condition called *haploidy*. The male cell will have either an X or a Y sex chromosome; as distinct from the female cell which carries only an X sex chromosome, e.g.:

	Sperm Gamete				*Ovum Gamete*			=	*Zygote*
	(22	+	X)	+	(22	+	X)	=	*female*
OR	(22	+	Y)	+	(22	+	X)	=	*male*

OR depicted in another fashion:

	Male		Female		Zygote
Gametes	(Sperm)	+	(ovum)	=	(fertilized egg)
Chromos	23	+	23	=	46
	(22 + X)	+	(22 + X)	=	44 + XX (female)
	(22 + Y)	+	(22 + X)	=	44 + XY (male)

There are several procedures used prenatally to determine the presence of fetal anomalies. They are ultrasound, amniocentesis with analysis of the fluid, chorionic villi sampling (CVS), maternal alpha-feto-protein concentrations (AFP), fetoscopy, and DNA analysis.

These procedures may be described as follows:
1) *Ultrasound (US)* — the use of these high-frequency energy waves can delineate the structural outline of the fetus by reflection of the energy. Thus a fetal anomaly, such as hydrocephalus, would be apparent.
2) *Amniocentesis* — a sample of amniotic fluid is aspirated from the amniotic cavity in order that the fetal somatic cells present may be cultured (developed) and their chromosomes studied. This procedure is usually performed about the 14th to 16th week of pregnancy. Under local skin anesthesia, a puncture site is prepared on the abdomen over the uterus. A needle is inserted at this site, and penetrates through the abdominal and uterine walls into the amniotic cavity. By means of a syringe about 20 cc. of fluid is withdrawn. The mean volume of fluid at 16 weeks is about 200 cc., and at 20 weeks it is about 400 cc. A complete turnover in volume can occur in about 3 hours. The number of cells at 16 weeks is about 12,000/cc. The culture fails in about 2% of the cases. With the use of ultrasound (US), the entrance of the needle may be guided, and the US will also show the location of the placenta. There are risks to the procedure involving bleeding, and inadvertent puncture of fetal or maternal tissues with resultant damage to these

tissues. There is an excess risk of 5% that something serious will go wrong after this procedure, compared to a pregnancy where this was not done. A recent study showed that out of 2,219 cases there was a fetal loss of 63 (2.84%). The minimum risk of amniocentesis-related fetal death has been estimated to be in the range of 0.06 to 0.09%. There have been studies concerning the occurrence of psychological problems associated with this procedure, e.g., hostility and anxiety.

3) *Chorionic Villi Sampling (CVS)* — this procedure, which is still at the stages of clinical trials[8], may either replace or be an adjunct to amniocentesis. This painless procedure is performed between the 7th and 12th weeks of pregnancy. Under the guidance of US, a plastic catheter containing a flexible aluminum obturator is passed through the vaginal and cervical canals up to the edge of the chorionic villi. This is the outer edge of the placenta, the so-called chorion laeve, which eventually is destined to disintegrate. About 30 milligrams of tissue is removed by suction from this area. This material is used for a chromosomal analysis which takes about ten hours. As the cells are composed of the same type of cells as the fetus, the material may also be used for DNA analysis and other chemical studies. The advantages of this method are many. It can be done in early pregnancy, usually about the 7th to 12th week; the analysis can be done within a few hours; it can be done through the cervical canal without anesthesia; and it can be done without purposely perforating the membranes. As far as complications are concerned, the magnitude of CVS risk is not known at this time. Abortion may occur in 1 to 3% of the cases, but since the procedure is being done at an early pregnancy, it may be difficult to distinguish from a spontaneous abortion. There are other potential risks such as bleeding, infection, lacerations, growth retardation, and intrauterine death of the fetus.

4) *Fetoscopy* — this involves the passage of a small tube (fetoscope) through the cervical canal to visualize the scalp veins of the fetus. Blood samples can be drawn from these vessels. The instrument can also be used for CVS sampling. The risk of adverse effects is about 3-5%.

5) *Maternal alpha-feto-protein (AFP)* — this is a laboratory test done on the blood serum of the mother. A rise from the normal amount suggests a fetal anomaly.

6) *DNA analysis* — this is a laboratory analysis of this nucleic acid which is present in the nuclei of the somatic cells, and is used to detect any abnormalities in its composition.

It is estimated that there are about 3400 Mendelian genetic defects that may be genetically transmitted. However, pin-pointing the defective gene, or its deficient protein, has been achieved in only 280 instances. Several are amenable to treatment, or correction, during or after pregnancy. Other statistics show that about 15% of newborns have a hereditary disorder of some severity. Also, 25% of hospital beds, usually institutional, are occupied by persons with some degree of genetic defect. There is a risk of about 3% that any baby born will have a birth defect, regardless of adverse genetic history. One-third of neonatal deaths are due to birth defects. One of every 50 children has a physical defect, or some degree of mental retardation, resulting from a genetic anomaly. Large numbers of pediatric hospital admissions are associated with genetic defects. Therefore, prenatal diagnosis and genetic counseling can reduce the tremendous burden of genetic disease by reassurance and guidance to those at risk with this problem. The use of the previously cited diagnostic procedures, plus a thorough genetic history, will provide a good basis for the diagnosis of suspected genetic defects.

Genetic Counseling — there are five major indications concerning those needing help:

1) *maternal age* — there are about 73% in this category having an age of 35 or over. The likelihood of diagnosing genetic anomalies is 1:180 at age 35. This figure exceeds the generally accepted risk of abortion, or fetal death after amniocentesis, which risk is about 1:200. Down's syndrome has been found to be the most common defect. At age 30 the risk is about 1:900; at age 35 it is 1:360; and at age 40 it is 1:109. The paternal contribution in an advanced age may involve one-quarter of the cases.

2) *prior chromosomal anomaly* (neural tube defect) — the risk of recurrence is about 1-2%, e.g., spina bifida.

3) *parental translocation carrier* — 1:500 is a carrier of balanced chromosomal translocation. This means that the portions of two or more chromosomes are interchanged without a duplication or deficiency of genetic information. These carriers are phenotypically (the chromosomal makeup) normal, but may produce genetically "unbalanced" offspring.

4) *single gene* — these are X-linked disorders such as hemophilia, Duchenne muscular dystrophy, and GGPD deficiency. They carry a recurrence risk of about 25%. More than 100 disorders can be diagnosed prenatally by means of cellular enzyme analysis for abnormal lipids, carbohydrate, mucopolysaccharides, and amino-acid metabolites.

5) *family history of neural defects* — amniocentesis or CVS, or both, is recommended when the risk of such a defect equals or exceeds 1%. In borderline cases US and AFP may also be used.

Another important aspect of counseling involves the liability to a physician when he neglects to point out the possibility of a genetic defect occurring. In the event of the delivery of an infant with a previously unsuspected defect, the physician must present such information, at the earliest possible time, to the parents. He should also arrange to have a meeting at a later date to discuss the situation. The potential burden for the care of an affected fetus should be communicated effectively, although the burden itself is an interpretation for the parents to estimate. At present this issue has become a moot point.

Tests done prenatally should be explained to the parents, and a letter of the results, risks, etc. should be sent to them. Even in the case where the parents refuse the option of prenatal studies, the record should reflect the offer made to perform such tests, especially in the case of suspected sickle-cell anemia, or Tay-Sachs disease. The necessity for such precautions arises from the increasing number of lawsuits involved, although verbal explanations concerning defects should always be a customary procedure.

A draft report, approved in 1982 by the President's Commission for the Study of Ethical Problems and Biomedical and Behavioral Research, was generally optimistic about the role that genetic screening could have in reducing birth defects and combating disease. However, it also expressed concern that patients need to be protected from potential abuses of the procedure. Briefly, the following recommendations were made.

1) genetic information should not be shared with third parties without the explicit consent of the party screened. The only exception would be to the relatives who would suffer serious harm if such information were withheld.

2) adoption laws should be changed to aid genetic counselors, such as physicians, in conveying pertinent information about serious genetic risks between adoptees and their biologic families.

3) mandatory genetic screening programs are justified only when voluntary testing proves inadequate to prevent serious harm to the defenseless, e.g., children.

4) use of amniocentesis for gender selection should be discouraged.

5) disclosure of sensitive incidental findings, such as maternity or diagnosis of an XY female, should begin with a presumption in favor of disclosure, and then be decided on a case-by-case basis.

6) genetic curricula should be developed for students in elementary school through the university level; and existing postgraduate programs should be upgraded.

7) genetic history-taking should be required from men donating sperm for artificial insemination; and such information should be provided to women undergoing AIV.

8) screening programs should be subjected to strict quality control.

One of the more controversial applications of genetic testing involve, e.g., the screening of applicants for jobs where they may be susceptible to industrial hazards, and the denial of employment based on the results of the testing. At present there are no good tests or systems ready to be introduced into the workplace. Such tests are bound to come however. As an extreme example: there would be general agreement that a person with hemophilia should not be employed as a butcher.

GENE THERAPY

The potential uses of genetic technology for therapy in humans has been classified as follows:[1,9]

1) *Somatic cell therapy* — this refers to the attempt to treat a discrete population of the patient's body cells, other than the reproductive cells, in order to alter the functioning of a defective gene (or eventually replace it) and thus cure the disease at its roots. It involves changes limited to the person being treated. At the present time, only the first step of cloning the normal gene, is technologically feasible.

2) *Germ-line cell (reproductive cells) therapy* — this is an academically proposed intervention in which the altered gene would affect not only the individual, but that individual would pass the altered gene to his or her offspring.

3) *Enhancement genetic engineering* — this refers to the insertion of a gene, or several genes, to produce a characteristic desired by the individual, e.g., hair color, larger muscles, sharper memory.

4) *Eugenic genetic engineering* — this refers to the systematic, preferential breeding of superior individuals (genotypes). It involves the attempt to intervene genetically to select for character traits, intelligence, various talents, etc. (positive eugenics).

The latter three of these potential uses of genetic therapy involve ethical issues of great complexity and magnitude. These issues should be viewed in the light of the following concerns: a) the *criterion* for judging genetic interventions; b) the *values* involved; and c) the *procedural method.*

In the Glossary there are several examples of genetic syndromes presented. There are also numerous books available as an aid to genetic counseling which statistically analyze the possibilities and percentages of the occurrence of defects to which a certain couple might be subject.

References

1. "Genetic Technology and Our Common Future." McCormick, Richard, S.J.: America, Apr. 27, 1985.
2. O. T. Avery, et al, Rockefeller Univ.
3. Francis H. C. Hicks, James D. Watson.
4. Johns Hopkins Univ.
5. Paul Berg, Stanford Univ.
6. Stanford Univ. and U. Calif.
7. Robert F. Weaver, Univ. of Kansas.
8. "Comparative Study of CVS and Amniocentesis for Prenatal Diagnosis"; Dept. of Human Genetics, Yale Univ. Sch. Med.: April 11, 1985.
9. Human Genetic Engineering; Hearings before the Sub-Committee on Investigations and Oversight of the House Committee on Science and Technology, 1982.

Chapter IV

A. EXPERIMENTING ON HUMAN SUBJECTS

— Informed Consent

(For the ethical aspects, see the first part of this Manual.)

The classification of experimental methods used on human subjects may be considered as follows:[1]

1) *therapeutic experiments* — these are considered to be of medical benefit to the subject. They are also designated as diagnostic, curative, or preventive.

2) *non-therapeutic experiments* — these are primarily research in nature, and are aimed at benefiting persons other than the subject.

3) *borderline experiments* — these are a combination of the previous two, and are often used on pilot groups, such as in the development of influenza and polio vaccines.

A *key basis* for making a judgment relative to medical ethics in human experimentation lies in the principle of reasonably free and adequately informed consent. Basically, experimentation requires a) the informed consent of the subject b) a potential of benefit to the subject and c) a sound scientific basis for the procedure.

In certain instances there are occasions where hazards may be unknown; or the disclosure of all possible hazards might so terrify the subject that he or she may be unwilling to submit to an experimental procedure which has a high prospect of being beneficial; or the subject may not be capable of grasping all pertinent and known factors. Because of this, the American Medical Association (AMA) has stated that there are exceptional circumstances where certain information may be withheld from the patient. This is thought to be especially true when the disclosure of information concerning the nature of a drug, or experimental procedures or risks, would be expected to materially affect the health of the patient, and would be detrimental to his/her best interests.

Proxy Consent may become an issue when a person is in the position of being a "moral agent," and thus a bearer of moral obligations. These obligations may pose problems in the case of non-therapeutic experiments.

Retrospective studies, in contradistinction from prospective studies, are usually of no concern in that they involve a review of work that is already accomplished. An exception might be in the case where a question of the invasion of privacy is raised.

Informed Consent

The concept of informed consent, in British Common Law, developed along two paths within the civil law; the tort of *battery*, and the tort of *negligence*. In the United States, the adaptation to Common Law has held, since 1905, that physicians are negligent if they do not have their patient's consent before proceeding with medical treatment. Some courts directed the evolution of the doctrine of consent along the path of negligence. The legal reason for this direction is rooted in the concept that battery is intentional, and negligence is unintentional.[2]

The term "informed consent" was not used in the U.S. until 1957. The general rule is that patients must give consent for any treatment. But, in order for it to be valid, consent must be based on knowledge that is not in the possession of most patients. Therefore, physicians are legally bound to give the following information to their patients: the nature of the ailment, the course of the proposed treatment, the probability of a desirable outcome, the alternate forms of available treatment (including none), and the risk of undesirable results. Different states have different rules to determine the sufficiency of information. Generally, the adequacy is based on either the *customary disclosure practices* by reasonable physicians in the community; or the *patient materiality standard* (the informational needs of the patient).

All jurisdictions recognize situations that make disclosures unnecessary. These exceptions include:

1) the patient has foreknowledge of the hazard (a commonly known risk).

2) the patient voluntarily waives the right to be told of the risk.

3) the patient would have agreed to the treatment whether or not a particular risk was known.

4) the hazard is not a reasonably foreseeable result of a properly performed appropriate procedure.

5) complete disclosure of the hazards would be harmful to the best interests of the patient — the so-called *therapeutic privilege.*

6) the patient is either mentally or legally incompetent.

7) an emergency necessitates intervention to prevent death or permanent injury.

In discussing informed consent,[3] one physician stated that he sees a problem developing in the medical profession regarding this issue. The truth is often harsh and even harmful; it can leave one devoid of hope and open to despair. The doctor must be honest with his patient, answer all questions truthfully, and must volunteer information that the patient needs to know, even if no questions are asked. It is also the physician's responsibility to withhold, as far as possible, information which might be harmful to the patient. Unless the patient insists (in which case, of course, the basic rule applies, and he must be told), there is really no reason for him to know explicit details of an operating procedure; or to be made fully aware of every conceivable danger in his situation. An extremely suggestible patient might even develop certain side-effects from medication just because he has heard that they are possible. Medically, every patient is entitled to enough information to make possible his informed consent. The patient is best served when the doctor tells him what he needs to know in order to decide whether to accept the diagnosis and thereby come to grips with the results of surgery or treatment. Of course, a patient may justifiably seek other opinions, and may ultimately reject the advice of the doctors. Such is his right; but he should not be making his decision with his mind so cluttered as to cloud his perspective. On the other hand, in the case where a patient refuses a type of treatment which is commonplace practice, and he fails to improve, he may be considered to be noncompliant. There is a time-honored ethical and legal maxim in noncompliance — "one who knowingly and willingly brings on an adverse situation is not wronged" (*scienti et volenti non fit iniuria*).

A professor of medicine states that hospital residents are very interested in discussing the ethical, as well as the medical, viewpoint of therapy.[4] Ethics is becoming another subspeciality of medicine, and there is need for training in the principles of the subject. The principle that patients should be told the truth stands as a valid doctrine. The principle that a patient's rights require consent to treatment, or nontreatment, is also valid and should be respected.

Problems arise most often in patients with terminal malignancy. Patients have a right to know, but they don't always want to know. A patient will frequently discuss the hopelessness of his situation with nurses and family, but rarely with his doctor. No matter how much patients admit to understanding the gravity of their situations, often they do not want to give up hope. Nevertheless, all questions should be answered truthfully; but, by not asking the important question, the patient is telling the physician something. Silence can be more eloquent than speech.

Individualization in therapy is vital, including the application of ethical principles. The ethical issue here involves a hierarchy of valid principles. It is right and important to tell the truth to patients; and to have the patient make the decisions regarding acceptance of his therapy, or the withholding of therapy. But there is another principle that deserves a higher priority on the scale of ethical care. It is, "Above all, do no harm" (*primum non nocere*).

The basic concept that patients should be fully informed about, participate in, and give their consent for, medical treatment is valid. Physicians should communicate and consult with patients, and assume responsibility for properly performing medical procedures. Patients should make decisions about their bodies, and assume responsibility for the risks inherent in such procedures.

Most physicians are conscientious about discussing conditions, alternatives, procedures and risks with their patients. But many fail to document properly what they have said and done. The written record is of paramount importance, especially in cases where a malpractice suit ensues.

B. RIGHTS OF HUMAN BEINGS (PERSONS)

Because of the nature of medical practice, ethical decisions encompass the whole life-cycle, starting before conception, extending from fetus to newborn, and continuing on to death.[5] The complexities of decision-making have been increased, owing to scientific innovations of recent years, e.g., intrauterine fertilization, prenatal diagnosis of fetal abnormalities, fetal surgery, total life-support for the very sick newborn, maintenance of adult life even after brain death — these extraordinary procedures often create ethical dilemmas for patients, families and health-care providers. Often involved are those who can't participate in the decision making, i.e., the fetus, the newborn, and the terminally ill adult. The mentally retarded are similarly excluded. Arising in the middle of these life-and-death situations are always the questions of cost, availability, and consumption of medical resources, not to mention the "quality of life." The real ethical problems eventuate into deciding who will be treated, who "will be allowed to die" (not treated), who pays (the family, the public, or the government), and who decides (to treat or not). Also who, and under what circumstances, should others than the doctor or patient be involved.

Fetal Surgery

The practice of fetal surgery (or intrauterine surgery) is still highly experimental. Up to early 1985, fewer than 200 fetuses had undergone surgery in-utero, and the results were highly variable. The conditions which showed beneficial promise included heart failure due to fetal arrhythmias, deficiency states due to anemia, and hypothyroidism. Also, anatomic lesions such as urethral obstruction with bilateral hydronephrosis, obstructive hydrocephalus, and diaphragmatic hernia. The transfusion of packed cells to the fetus for certain blood problems is no longer experimental.

Patient selection is a problem. In the case of obstruction in the urinary tract, a shunt or catheter is placed from the bladder to the amniotic cavity to divert the urinary flow. Of 52 fetuses operated upon, only 23 survived. In the case of hydrocephalus, a shunt is placed from the lateral ventricle (brain) to the amniotic cavity to divert buildup of fluid which could increase the intracranial pressure and result in brain damage. Of 26 fetuses having this surgery, 21 survived; but 7 were severely retarded, and 3 showed developmental delay.

There are many other conditions which are best treated after delivery, such as bowel obstructions, neural tube defects (spina bifida), and various cysts and tumors. Some of these defects may require Caesarean Section because of the increased size of the fetal structure, such as with conjoined twins and large tumors.

References

1. "Human Existence, Medicine, and Ethics," Dr. William E. May.
2. "Informed Consent: a confusing concept," Daniel K. Roberts, M.D., PhD.; Contemp. OB-GYN, May 1985.
3. "Do Patients Need To Know Everything," Lester Karafin, M.D.; Hospital Tribune, Dec. 7, 1983.
4. "On Telling Patients the Truth," Alfred Jay Bollet, M.D.; Resident and Staff Physician, Jan. 1984.
5. Editorial, John L. Queenan, M.D.; Contem. OB-GYN, Jul 1983.

Glossary of Medical Terms

(Relating to Medical Aspects of Bioethics)

This glossary has been assembled to provide ready access to and understanding of some of the terms encountered in the area of technological reproduction.

The reference for several conditions of abnormal genetic origin can be found under "Syndromes."

For the ethical aspects, see Part I.

Leo T. Duffy, M.D.
(July 1987)

A

abortion (L. aborto, to miscarry). The giving of birth to an embryo or fetus prior to the stage of viability at about 20 weeks of gestation (fetus weighs less than 400-500 grams). A distinction is made between a. and premature birth; premature infants are those born after the stage of viability has been reached, but before full term. Additional classifications are:

spontaneous a., (natural) — where no medical or surgical means have been used.

inevitable a., — where the membranes rupture spontaneously, and the uterine cervix is dilating.

habitual a., — where there have been three or more spontaneous consecutive embryonic or fetal losses.

incomplete a., — where only portions of the conceptus have been passed.

complete a., — where the embryo, placenta and membranes have all been passed.

   missed a., — where the fetus dies in-utero, and is retained for two or more months. This is the situation where a lithopedion (stone/small child) may occur.

   threatened a., — where cramps, pains and vaginal bleeding occur.

   induced a., — where evacuation of the uterine cavity is brought on by drugs or mechanical means. The term "therapeutic" is also used when the induction is performed for the sake of the mother's health. This is a classification which raises moral/medical/legal questions.

adenine. A purine found in RNA and DNA, and various nucleotides in the body.

alpha-feto-protein (AFP). This is a laboratory test done on blood serum from the mother. A rise from the normal suggests a fetal anomaly.

amenorrhea (G. a-priv + men, month + rhoia, flow). Absence or abnormal cessation of the menses.

amnion (G. the membrane around the fetus, AMNI-). The innermost of the two membranes enveloping the fetus in-utero.

amniocentesis (AMNI + G. kentesis, puncture). Aspiration of amniotic fluid usually by needle puncture through the abdominal and uterine walls.

arginine. One of the amino-acids occurring among the hydrolysis products of protein (see DNA).

arrhythmia (G. a-priv + rhythmos, rhythm). Irregularity; loss of rhythm; denoting especially an irregularity of the heartbeat.

B

basal temperature. The body temperature, usually taken in the early morning, and used in the sympto-thermal method for determining the occurrence of ovulation.

blastocyst (G. blastos, germ + kystis, bladder). The modified blastula stage of mammalian embryos. Occurs during the cleavage germ layer formation in the development of the embryo.

brain death. (see Harvard criteria).

C

catamenia. See menses.

cervical mucus. A viscid secretion produced by the endocervical glands of the uterus; a hydrogel which changes its viscosity under the hormonal influence of estrogen and progesterone.

cervix (L. neck) uteri. The lower part of the uterus which is visible within the vagina.

cervical os. The opening in the cervix which leads to the canal opening into the uterine cavity.

chlamydia trachomatis. (G. chlamys, a mantle + G. trachys, rough, harsh). A microorganism responsible for the most common sexually transmitted infections.

chorion (G. chorion, membrane enclosing the fetus. CHORI). The outermost of the fetal membranes.

chorionic villi sampling (CVS) (L. shaggy hair (of beasts). Biopsy of a small portion of the vascular processes of the chorion of the embryo which enter into the formation of the placenta. The tissue is examined to determine the chromosomal characteristics (karyotype) of the fetus.

chromosome (G. chroma, color + soma, body). A body in the cell nucleus that is the bearer of genes.

cleavage. The series of cell divisions occurring in the ovum immediately following fertilization.

clomiphene citrate (CLOMID). A synthetic preparation used to stimulate follicle-ripening in the ovaries.

clone (G. klon, slip, cutting used for propagation). A colony or group of organisms which have arisen from a single individual as a result of asexual reproduction.

cloning. An exact, genetic duplication of a single individual by the transfer of chromosomes from a body cell of an individual to an ovum from which the existing chromatin material (chromosomes) has been previously removed.

coitus (L. co-eo, pp. -itus, to come together). Copulation, coition, sexual union.

coitus interruptus. Withdrawal of the male organ before ejaculation; onanism.

conception (L. conceptio). The act of conceiving, or becoming pregnant; the fecundation of the ovum.

condom. A sheath or cover for the penis for use in the prevention of conception, or of infection, during coitus.

contraception. The prevention of conception or impregnation, usually by the use of hormonal, chemical or mechanical means.

cornu (uterine). (L. horn). The upper (fundus), bilateral portion of the uterus where the Fallopian tubes attach.

corpus (L. gen. corporis, pl. corpora, the body). The main part of an organ (e.g. uterus), or other anatomical structure, as distinguished from the caput (head), or cauda (tail).

corpus luteum. The yellow endocrine body formed in the ovary in the site of a ruptured ovarian follicle after the release of the ovum. It secretes the hormone progesterone.

curretage. A scraping of the interior of a cavity, e.g. the uterus, with a sharp-edged instrument (curet).

cytosine. A pyrimidine base found among hydrolysis products of nucleic acid (see DNA).

D

decidua (L. deciduus, falling off (qualifying membrana, membrane understood), e.g. shedding of endometrial tissue during menses.

deoxyribonucleic acid (DNA). A nucleic acid present in the nuclei of animal and vegetable cells; it is a macromolecule of the same order of complexity as protein molecules; in combining with protein (DNA protein), it makes up the auto-producing component of chromosomes and of many viruses. It is perhaps the nearest thing to a fundamental component of living tissue. It contains the nucleotides adenine (A), cytosine (C), guanine (G), and thymine (T), — the "genetic language."

dilation (L. dilate, pp dilatatus, to spread out, dilate). The enlargement of a cavity, canal, or opening.

dilation and curettage (D&C). A procedure involving dilation of the cervical canal to facilitate the insertion of a curette which is used to scrape the uterine lining (endometrium) — as in induced abortion.

dilation and evacuation (D&E). Similar to a D&C, except that the evacuation of the uterine contents is usually done by suction.

diploid (G. diplous, double + eidos, resemblance). Relating to the pair of chromosomes in the body cells, and mature germ cells, of the great majority of animals and plants. Haploid refers to one-half that number.

double helix. The characteristic double coil formation of strands of genes within the chromosomal structure.

ductus deferens. The secretory duct of the testicle, running as a continuum of the epididymis to the prostatic urethra where it terminates as the ejaculatory duct.

E

early prenatal karyotyping (EPK). A still experimental test to detect fetal anomalies using a standard maternal blood sample. The fetal trophoblasts found therein are genetically identical to other fetal cells. The test may be done at 7-8 weeks gestation.

ectopic (G. ek, out of, + topos, place). In pregnancy it refers to a location elsewhere than within the uterine cavity.

ejaculation (L. ejaculatio, JAC, Throw, hurl).
  premature e., — rapid termination of the sexual act on the part of the male.
  retrograde e., — (L. retro, backward + gradior, to go). The seminal fluid is directed back into the bladder due to a physical anomaly.

electroencephalograph (electro + G. encephalon, brain + grapho, to write). An apparatus consisting of a cathode ray oscillometer with saline leads on the scalp which record the alternating currents of the brain (encephalogram).

embryo (G. embryon, fr en, in + bryo, to be full, swell). An organism in the early stages of development; in man, from conception until approximately the end of the second month.

endometriosis. The ectopic occurrence of endometrial tissue, with infiltration of pelvic organs.

endometrium (G. endon, within + metra, uterus). The mucus membrane lining of the cavity of the uterus.

epididymis (Mod. L. ir G., fr epi, on + didymos, twin, in pl. testes). The first convoluted portion of the excretory duct of the testis. It merges into the vas deferens.

estrogen (G. oistros, mad desire + root GEN, to beget). A generic term for all substances which produce estrus (heat). Mainly, a hormone secreted by the ovarian follicles. Also synthetically prepared.

eugenics (G. nobility of birth, fr. eu, well + root GEN). The science which deals with the influences, especially prenatal, that tend to better the innate qualities of man; and to develop them to the highest degree by artificial selection.

    positive e. — embody efforts to improve genetic heritage, i.e., artificial insemination, IVF, sperm/ovum banks and genetic engineering.

    negative e. — method used to prevent transmission of genetically-induced disorders to a future generation, e.g., sterilization, abortion, and planned parenthood.

euthanasia (G. fr. eu, well + thanatos, death). A quiet, painless death. The intentional putting to death by artificial means of persons with incurable or painful disease.

    active e. — the directly willed inducement of death for merciful reasons; the "mercy killing."

    passive e. — allowing oneself, or another person, to die when the person is terminally ill, and there is no obligation to continue life-support (or death-prolonging) means because there is no reasonable hope of recovery.

experiment. A test or a trial.

    therapeutic e. — those which are considered to be of medical benefit to the subject. Also may be designated as diagnostic, curative, or preventive.

    non-therapeutic e. — those which are primarily research in nature, and are aimed at benefitting persons other than the subject.

    borderline e. — those which are a combination of the previous two, and are often utilized on pilot groups, such as in the development of "flu" and polio vaccines.

F

Fallopian tube (salpinx) (G. a trumpet). The tubal structures attached at each uterine cornu, and acting as the passageway for the ovum to enter the uterine cavity.

fecundity (L. fecundo, fruitful). The capacity for procreation.

fetoscopy. The introduction of an examining tube through the cervix in order to visualize the fetal scalp. Blood samples can be taken from the scalp veins.

fertile (L. fertilis; fero, to bear). Fruitful; capable of conceiving and bearing young. Denotes actual procreation.

fertilization. The penetration of the sperm cell into the ovum.

fetus (L. offspring). In man, the product of conception from the end of the eighth week to the moment of birth.

fibroid. See myoma.

fissure (L. fissio, a cleaving, fr findo, pp fissus, to cleave, FIS-). The act of splitting, e.g., amitotic division of a cell or its nucleus.

follicle (Graffian or ovarian). (L. folliculus, a small sac). One of the vascular bodies in the ovary containing an ovum.

frigidity. Sexual coldness.

fundus (uterine). The upper rounded extremity of the uterus above the openings of the Fallopian tubes.

G

gamete (G. gametes, husband; gamete, wife). One of two cells undergoing true conjugation. In heredity any germ cell, whether ovum, spermatozoon, or pollen cell.

gene (root, GEN, beget). The functional unit of heredity. It occupies a specific place or locus on a chromosome; is capable of reproducing itself exactly at each cell division, and is capable of directing the formation of an enzyme or other protein. The gene, as a functional unit, probably consists of a discrete segment of a giant DNA molecule containing the proper number of purine (adenine and guanine), and pyrimidine (cytosine and thymine) bases in the correct sequence for coding amino-acids. Gene's normally occur in pairs in all cells except gametes, as a consequence of the fact that all chromosomes are paired except the sex chromosomes (X and Y) of the male.

genetic engineering. A process of manipulating or altering the genetic structure of a body cell.

genetics. The branch of science that deals with natural development — the study of heredity.

gestation (L. gestatio, fr gesto, pp. gestatus, to bear). Pregnancy; fetation.

gland (L. glans, acorn. GLAN-). A secreting organ.

    endocrine g., — ductless gland; the main activity of which is the production of an internal secretion, e.g., thyroid, ovary.

    exocrine g., — produces an external secretion, e.g., salivary.

gonad (Mod. L., fr., G. gene, seed). A germ gland; sexual gland as ovary and testicle.

gonadotrophin. A gonad stimulating hormone, as from the anterior pituitary gland.

    human chorionic g., (HCG) — A hormone prepared from the urine of pregnant women.

    human menopausal g., (HMG) — A hormone prepared from the urine of post-menopausal women.

guanine. A purine occurring among the the hydrolysis products of nucleic acid (see DNA).

H

haploid. See diploid.

Harvard criteria. A definition of brain death which equates with (1) lack of spontaneous respiration, (2) no brain activity showing on an electroencephalogram, checked by one observer, and then by another 24 hours later, (3) no reflexive response to external stimuli. All these are in the absence of intoxicants, or severe fever.

heterologous (G. heteros, different + logos, ratio, relation). The phrase "heterologous artificial fertilization" means the techniques used to obtain human conception artificially by the use of gametes coming from at least one vendor other than the spouse.

homologous (G. homos, same + logos, word, ratio, relation). The technique used to obtain a human conception using the gametes of the two spouses joined in marriage.

hormone (G. hormon, pres. part. of hormao, to rouse or set in motion). A chemical substance, formed in one organ or part of the body, and carried in the blood stream to another or body part which it stimulates to functional activity.

hospice. A program which involves the spiritual, intellectual, physical and emotional support of a terminally ill patient, and his/her family, throughout the illness and bereavement period.

human chorionic gonadotrophin (HCG). A hormone that will maintain luteal function, and that is produced by the placental trophoblastic cells. It is prepared from the urine of pregnant women.

hydatidiform mole. A vesicular or polycystic intrauterine mass formed by degeneration of the partly developed fertilized ovum.

hydramnios (G. hydor, water). The presence of an excessive amount of amniotic fluid.

hydrocele (G. hydrokele, fr hydor, water + kele, hernia). A collection of serous fluid in a sacculated cavity, such as the tunica of the testis.

hydrocephalus (G. hydor, water + kephale, head). A condition, usually congenital, marked by an excessive accumulation of fluid in the cerebral ventricles.

hydronephrosis (G. nephros, kidney). Dilation of the pelvis and calyces of one or both kidneys in consequence of obstruction to flow of urine.

hymen (G. hymen, membrane). A thin crescentic or annular membranous fold partly or wholly occluding the vaginal external orifice in the virgin.

hyperprolactinemia. An excessive amount of the hormone, prolactin, of the anterior lobe of the hypophysis which normally stimulates the secretion of milk.

hypospadias (G. fr. hypospao, to draw away from under). A developmental anomaly characterized by a defect in the urethral wall whereby the canal opening is located on the under surface of the penis.

hysterectomy (G. hystera, uterus + ectome, excision). Removal of the body of the uterus. A subtotal h. would be the removal of the body of the uterus leaving the cervix in situ. The removal of the entire uterus, plus the tubes and the ovaries is called a hystero-salpingo-oophorectomy.

I

implantation. The attachment of the fertilized ovum (blastocyst) to the endometrium, and its embedding into the compact layer, occurring six to seven days after fertilization.

impotence. Weakness, lack of power; specifically, lack of ability in the male to copulate.

infertility. Diminished or absent fertility.

insemination (L. in-semino, pp. -atus, to sow or plant in, fr. semen, seed) The depositing of seminal fluid within the vagina; normally introduced during coitus.

    artificial i. — the introduction of the semen of the husband, or of another, into the vagina otherwise than through the coital act.

    heterologous i. (AIV) — artificial, with semen from a vector who is not the woman's husband.

    homologous i. (AIH) — artificial, using the husband's semen.

intrauterine device (IUD). Any small, variously shaped piece, made usually of polyethylene, for insertion into the uterus as a continuous contraceptive. Some are infused with a chemical, such as copper; or contain a contraceptive hormone.

intrauterine surgery. A surgical procedure performed on the fetus usually during the third trimester of pregnancy.

in-vitro (L. in glass). Performed in a test tube, or glass dish.

in-vitro fertilization (IVF). The artificial insemination of an ovum located in a special growth medium in a glass receptacle.

in-vivo (L. in the living being). Vital chemical processes in the living body, as distinguished from those occurring in a test tube.

K

karyotype. The chromosomal characteristics of an individual, or of a cell line.

L

labia (L. labium, lip). Any lip-shaped structure, e.g., the outer vaginal folds.

laparoscopy (G. lapara, flank. loins + skopeo, to view). An examination of the abdominal cavity.

laparotomy (G. lapara + tome, incision). Incision through any part of the abdominal wall. As in celiotomy (G. koilia, belly + tome, incision).

low tubal ovum transfer (LTOT). A procedure used in

problems of infertility whereby an ovum is obtained by laparoscopy, and transferred into the tube or ovary.

luteinizing hormone. An anterior pituitary hormone which stimulates the transformation of ovarian follicles (and their theca interna cells) into a corpus luteum after ovulation.

M

meiosis (G. meiosis, a lessening). The special process of cell division that results in the formation of gametes, consisting of two nuclear divisions in rapid succession that result in the formation of four gametocytes, each containing half the number of chromosomes found in the somatic cells of the body.

menarche (G. men, month + arche, beginning). The establishment of the menstrual cycle function.

menopause. Permanent cessation of the menses.

menses (menstruation; menstrual cycle) (L. pl. of mensis, month). A periodic, physiological vaginal bleeding, usually at four week intervals, having its source from the endometrial lining of the uterus.

microcephaly (G. mikros, small + kephale, head). Abnormal smallness of the head, with a skull capacity below 1350 cc.

mitosis (G. mitos, thread). The usual process of cell reproduction consisting of a sequence of modification of the nucleus (prophase, prometaphase, metaphase, anaphase, and telophase) that result in the formation of two daughter cells with exactly the same chromosomes and DNA content as that of the original cell.

mittelschmerz (Ger., middle pain). Abdominal pain occurring at the time of ovulation, resulting from irritation of the pelvic peritoneum by the bleeding from the ovulation site on the ovary.

morula (mod L dim. of L. morus, mulberry). The mass of

blastomeres resulting from the early cleavage division of the zygote.

myoma. A benign tumor of the muscular tissue, as in the uterus. It is also called a fibroid, although this tumor is composed of fibrous tissue.

N

Natural Family Planning. A method used to avoid conception, by abstinence at the physiological time of ovulation, e.g., the sympto-thermal method (q.v.).

neural tube (G. neuron, nerve). A nervous system channel.

nucleic acid. A family of substances found in chromosomes, mitochondria, and viruses; now thought to be the ultimate carriers of physical characteristics, and to control the enzyme pattern characteristic of the cells of which they form a part. With proteins they form nucleoproteins.

nucleoprotein. One of a group of conjugated proteins consisting of a compound of similar proteins with nucleic acid, e.g., chromosomes, mitochondria, and viruses.

nucleoside. A compound of a sugar with a purine or pyrimidine base.

nucleotide. A hydrolysis product of nucleic acid, usually composed of carbon, hydrogen, nitrogen, and oxygen.

O

oligospermia (G. oligos, little + sperma, seed). Deficient secretion or expulsion of semen.

orchidectomy (orchiectomy) (G. orchis, tesis + ektome, excision). Castration; removal of one or both testes.

ovary (L. ovum, egg). One of two reproductive, female glands containing the ova or germ cells.

ovulation. The escape of an ovum from the Graafian follicle.

ovum (gen. ovi. pl. ova; L. egg). The female sexual cell from which, when fertilized by union with the male spermatozoon, a new individual is developed.

P

parthenogenesis (G. aparthenos, virgin; genesis, procreation). A form of nonsexual reproduction, or agamogenesis in which the female reproduces its kind without fecundation by the male.

pelvic inflammatory disease (PID). An acute or chronic inflammation of the pelvic cavity, usually involving the tubes and contiguous structures. It is usually a result of bacterial (gonorrheal) infection, or of endometriosis.

peritonitis. Inflammation of the serous membrane lining of the abdominal cavity.

phenotype (G. phaino, to display + typos, model). In genetics, a group to which an individual may be assigned on the basis of one or more chromosomal characteristics that reflect genetic variations.

pituitary (hypophysis) (G. an undergrowth). A small two-lobed body at the base of the brain. It is an internal (endocrine) secreting gland furnishing gonadotrophic, thyrotrophic, adrenotrophic, prolactin, and growth-promoting principles (anterior lobe).

placenta (L. cake). The organ of metabolic interchange between fetus and mother. At term it averages about 1/6 to 1/7 the weight of the fetus; is disc-shaped; about 1 inch thick and 7 inches in diameter, and connects to the fetus by way of the umbilical cord. After delivery, the placenta, membranes, and attached cord are extruded as the "afterbirth."

progesterone. A steroid hormone believed to be the active principle of the corpus luteum of the ovary. It can also be isolated from the placenta; or synthetically prepared.

prostaglandins. These are synthetic 20 carbon compounds, two of which have been designated as PGF2a (injectable), and PGE2 (used as a vaginal suppository). One use is to stimulate uterine contractions to dilate the cervix, or to promote an abortion.

R

recombinant DNA. This has been produced by the combining of the DNA from two viruses. This substance then can be inserted into bacteria to reproduce or clone this foreign DNA.

restrictive enzyme. This has been discovered as a kind of molecular scissors used to slice DNA molecules.

S

saline, hypertonic. Salt (G. hypertonos, strained to the utmost). A solution of sodium chloride with greater osmotic pressure than blood.

segmentation-implantation. Seg., the series of cell divisions (cleavage) occurring in the ovum immediately following fertilization. Impl., the attachment of the fertilized ovum (blastocyst) to the endometrium by imbedding in the compact layer; occurring approximately eight days after fertilization of the ovum.

semen (L. semen (semin), seed). A mixture of the secretions of the testes, seminal vesicles, prostate and Cowper's glands, (seminal fluid).

seminal vesicles. Two folded, sacculated, glandular structures which are diverticulae of the ductus deferens. Their secretion is one of the components of the semen.

spermatozoon. (G. sperm, seed + zoon, animal). The male sexual cell.

spina bifida. A limited defect in the spinal column, consisting of the absence of the vertebral arches, through which the spinal membranes, with or without spinal cord tissue, protrude.

stenosis (G.). A narrowing of any canal; a stricture.

sterilization. The act or process of making any person or any thing infertile or barren.

stillbirth. Fetal death in utero.

surrogate (L. surrogare, to put in another's place); person who substitutes for another. As is used in surrogate motherhood where a mature female agrees to be artificially inseminated, and after delivery relinquish to adoptive parents.

surrogate embryo transfer. Artificial insemination of a female, with removal of the embryo at an early stage of development (5th to 7th day) by intrauterine flushing. The embryo is then transferred to the uterine cavity of the female who will carry the fetus to term and eventual delivery, and will be the mother.

surrogate mother — a female assuming the role of a mother in the biological development of a fetus. This role may involve the provision of an ovum, or may involve only the provision of the uterus as an incubator for the developing fetus.

sympto-thermal method. A method used in natural family planning to identify the time of ovulation by observing certain temperature, and other physical changes.

syndromes. (see last page of glossary)

T

technological reproduction. Procedures used to obtain human conception in a manner other than the sexual (coital) union of man and woman. Also called "artificial procreation" and/or "artificial fertilization."

thymine. A pyrimidine constituent of thymus nucleic acid (see DNA).

trait (fr. L. trahere, tractum, to draw). A characteristic.
    dominant t. — a character possessed by one of the parents of a hybrid which appears in the latter to the exclusion of a contrasted character (*recessive*) from the other parent.

transduction. The transfer of genetically determined properties between microorganisms through mediation of bacteriophage.

transformation. Metamorphosis; change of form and shape. Translocation.

translocation. The transposition of two segments between non-homologous chromosomes as a result of abnormal breakage, and refusion of reciprocal segments.

trisomy. State of an individual or cell containing an extra chromosome; instead of the normal pair of homologous chromosomes, there are three of a particular chromosome; in man, the state of a cell containing 47 normal chromosomes.

trophoblast. (G. trophe, nourishment + blastos, germ). The ectodermal cell layer covering the blastocyst which erodes the uterine mucosa and through which the embryo receives nourishment from the mother. It contributes to the formation of the placenta but not the embryo.

tubal ligation. Cutting and/or occluding the Fallopian tubes of the female with suture material or clips.

U

ultrasound. Energy waves (vibrations) similar to those of sound, but of higher frequencies, which are used to delineate deep structures by measuring the reflection or transmission of the ultrasound energy.

urea, hypertonic. Urea (G. ouran, urine). The chief end-product of nitrogen metabolism, excreted in human urine (altered to a hypertonic state).

urethra (G. ourethra, urethra). A canal leading from the bladder, and discharging the urine externally.

uterus. The womb; the hollow muscular organ in which the impregnated ovum is developed into the child. It is about 3 inches in length in the non-pregnant state. It consists of a main portion, the corpus; an elongated cervix or neck, at the extremity of which is the opening (the cervical os or mouth).

V

vagina (L. sheath). The genital canal in the female extending from the cervix to the vulva.

vaginismus. Painful spasm of the vaginal muscles preventing satisfactory coitus.

varicocele. (L. varix, a dilated vein. VAR + G. kele, tumor, hernia). A varicose enlargement of the veins of the spermatic cord.

vector (L. vector, a carrier). In the case of artificial insemination, the supplier of the seminal specimen (male), or the female ovum.

vendor. A person or agency that sells. This applies to third party individuals who supply either the sperm or ovum for the purpose of procreation.

viability (Fr. viabilite; L. vita, life). Capability of living; the state of being viable; usually connotes a fetus that has reached 500 grams in weight, and reached 20 gestational weeks.

virility (L. virilitas, manhood, fr. vir, man). The reproductive age in the man; manhood.

W, X, Y, Z

zona pellucida. Clear zone; a tough refractile, clear membrane enveloping the ovum.

zygote (G. zygotas, yoked). The individual produced by the fusion of two cells in true conjugation; the fertilized macrogamete.

Syndromes

syndrome [G., syndrone, a running together; (in med) a concurrence of symptoms, fr. syn, together + dromos, a running]. The aggregate of signs and symptoms associated with any morbid process, and constituting together the picture of the disease.

cystic fibrosis (of the pancreas). A generalized, inheritable disease of unknown cause; associated with dysfunction of all exocrine glands, including those that are mucus-producing.
Down's syndrome (mongolism). A syndrome of mental retardation with a variable constellation of physical abnormalities.
Duchennes syndrome. A subacute or chronic anterior spinal paralysis combined with multiple neuritis.
dwarfism. A condition of faulty development (of several varieties) that may be due to congenital failure of cartilage growth.
epiloia. Hypertrophic sclerosis of the cerebral cortex; associated with skin and kidney growths.
hemophilia. An inherited disorder of the blood marked by a permanent tendency to hemorrhage, spontaneous or traumatic, due to a defect in the blood coagulating power. A recessive trait carried by females, and affecting males.
Huntington's chorea [G. choreia, a choral dance, fr. choros, a dance]. A hereditary disorder (chronic) beginning usually between 20-50 years, characterized by choretic movements of face and extremities, and gradual loss of mental faculties.
phenylketonuria. A congenital deficiency of the phenylalanine hydroxylase (enzyme) allowing accumulation of p. metabolites resulting in brain damage, and other neurologic abnormalities.

pyloric stenosis [G. pyloros, a gatekeeper; the pylorus + stenosis, a narrowing]. Stricture or narrowing of the pyloric (stomach) outlet.

retinal aplasia. Failure of development of the optic retina.

sickle cell anemia. Hereditary, familial hemolytic anemia, peculiar to the black race.

Tay-Sach's disease. Amaurotic [G. amauros, dark, obscure] familial idiocy. Dominant in the Jewish race.

Turner's syndrome. Dwarfism, webbed neck, valgus of the elbows, amenorrhea and sexual infantilism; found in genetic males with absent sex chromatin.

Selected Bibliography

SPECIAL MAGISTERIAL SOURCES

Congregation for the Doctrine of the Faith, *The Gift of Life*, "Instruction on Respect for Human Life in its Origins and on the Dignity of Procreation: Replies to Certain Questions of the Day," 22 February 1987.

Pope John Paul II, *Familiaris Consortio.* Apostolic Exhortation on the Family in the Modern World, 22 November 1981.

Pope Paul VI, *Humanae Vitae.* Encyclical Letter. 25 July 1968.

Congregation for the Doctrine of the Faith, *Persona Humana* (Declaration on Certain Questions Pertaining to Sexual Ethics). 29 December 1975.

Vatican Council II, *Gaudium et Spes* (Pastoral Constitution on the Church in the Modern World), 7 December 1965.

Congregation for the Doctrine of the Faith, "The Letter to Bishops of the Catholic Church on the Pastoral Care of Homosexual Persons." 1 October 1986.

Pope Pius XII, *Address to Midwives*, 29 October 1951.

Pope Piux XI, *Casti Connubii* (Encyclical Letter on Christian Marriage. 31 December 1930.)

National Conference of Catholic Bishops, U.S.A. *Human Life in Our Day* (Pastoral Letter), 15 November 1968.

National Conference of Catholic Bishops, U.S.A. *To Live in Christ Jesus* (Pastoral Reflection on the Moral Life), 11 November 1976.

COMPILATION

Flannery, A., *Vatican Council II*, Vols. I and II, *Post Conciliar Documents;* and *More Post Conciliar Documents.* Northport, N.Y.: Costello, 1975 and 1982.

COMPLIATIONS AND BOOKS

John Paul II, *The Original Unity of Man and Woman.* Boston: St. Paul Editions, 1979.

_____, *Blessed are the Pure of Heart.* Boston: St. Paul Editions, 1983.

_____, *The Theology of Marriage and Celibacy*, Boston: St. Paul Editions, 1986.

Wojtyla, Karol, *Love and Responsibility*, New York: Farrar, Straus and Giroux, 1981.

_____, *The Jeweler's Shop*, New York, Random House, 1980.

GENERAL SOURCES

Dennehy, Raymond, "The Biological Revolution," in *Pope John Paul II Lecture Series in Bioethics*, Vol. I, *Perspectives in Bioethics*, ed., Francis J. Lescoe and David Q. Liptak: Cromwell, CT, Holy Apostles College and Seminary, 1983.

* *

Lawler, Ronald, "Critical Reflections on Current Bioethical Thinking," in *Pope John Paul II Lecture Series in Bioethics*, ed. Francis J. Lescoe and David Q. Liptak: Cromwell, CT, Holy Apostles College and Seminary, 1983.

May, William E., "Begotten, not Made," *In Pope John Paul II Lecture Series in Bioethics*, Vol. 1, *Perspectives in Bioethics:* ed. Francis J. Lescoe and David Q. Liptak. Cromwell, CT: Holy Apostles College and Seminary, 1983.

Lawler, Ronald, Joseph Boyle, and William E. May, *Catholic Sexual Ethics* (Huntinggon, Ind.: OSV, 1985).

Lawler, Ronald, et al. *The Teaching of Christ*, 2nd Edition, Huntington: OSV, 1983.

* *

Liptak, David Q., *Biblical-Catechetical Homilies.* Staten Island: Alba House, 1980.

Liptak, David Q., *The New Code and the Sacraments*, Vol. 1, Lake Worth: Sunday Publications, 1984.

* *

Lescoe, Francis J., *Existentialism With Or Without God.* Staten Island: Alba House, 1980.

May, William E., *Sex, Marriage, and Chastity.* Chicago: Franciscan Herald Press, 1981.

_____, *Human Existence, Medicine and Ethics*, Chicago: Franciscan Herald Press, 1977.

* *

Moral Theology Today, The Pope John Center, *Certitudes and Doubts*, St. Louis: The Pope John Center, 1984.

Technological Powers and the Person, ed. Albert S. Moraczewski, Donald G. McCarthy et al., St. Louis: The Pope John Center, 1983.

Handbook on Critical Sexual Issues, ed. Donald G. McCarthy and Edward J. Bayer, St. Louis: The Pope John Center, 1983 (Note: The Pope John Center is now located in Braintree, MA).

* *

Woznicki, Andrew N., *A Christian Humanism, Karol Wojtyla's Existential Personalism*. New Britain, CT: Mariel Publ., 1980.

Principles of Catholic Moral Life, ed. William E. May, Chicago: Franciscan Herald Press, 1980.

* *

PAMPHLETS

Albacete, Lorenzo. *Commentary*, Instruction on *Bioethics, Respect for Human Life*. Boston: St. Paul Editions, 1987.

De Marco, Donald. *Infertility and "In Vitro" Fertilization, Its Meaning and Morality*. Saskatchewan: Marian Press Ltd., 1985.